John Foxe

Twayne's English Authors Series

Arthur F. Kinney, Editor

University of Massachusetts, Amherst

TEAS 345

IOHANNES FOXVS.

Colligit ⟨et⟩ FOXVS Sanctorum gesta virorum
Digna facit Sanctis plurima martyribus.

Æ

JOHN FOXE
(1517–1587)
Courtesy of The Houghton Library,
Harvard Univeristy

John Foxe

By Warren W. Wooden

Marshall University

Twayne Publishers • Boston

John Foxe

Warren W. Wooden

Copyright © 1983 by G.K. Hall & Company
All Rights Reserved
Published by Twayne Publishers
A Division of G. K. Hall & Company
70 Lincoln Street
Boston, Massachusetts 02111

Book Production by John Amburg

Book Design by Barbara Anderson

Printed on permanent/durable acid-free
paper and bound in the United States of
America.

**Library of Congress Cataloging in
Publication Data**

Wooden, Warren W.
John Foxe.

(Twayne's English authors series;
TEAS 345)
Bibliography: p. 134
Includes index.
1. Foxe, John, 1517–1587
—Criticism and interpretation.
I. Title. II. Series.
PR2276.F7Z93 1983 272'.6'0924 82-15605
ISBN 0-8057-6830-0

Contents

About the Author

Warren W. Wooden received his B.A. from the University of North Carolina at Chapel Hill, his M.A. from the University of Mississippi, and his Ph.D. from Vanderbilt University. He is now professor of English at Marshall University. He has published numerous articles on Renaissance authors including Thomas More, Sir John Suckling, Michael Drayton, John Skelton, George Herbert, and Shakespeare. He is the author of the John Foxe bibliography in the "Recent Studies" series published in *English Literary Renaissance* and the editor of a facsimile edition of *The English Sermons of John Foxe.*

Editor's Foreword

The breadth and range of appeal of John Foxe's *Acts and Monuments* or *Book of Martyrs* in Renaissance England cannot be overestimated. From the ordinary citizen who knew it as one of the four chained books in cathedrals and parish churches to the great and near-great, such as Sir Francis Drake who took a copy around the world with him in 1577, Foxe's work met an enthusiastic reception in Protestant England. It rivaled the Bible in the sweep of its intention and accomplishment and in its massive influence on the thought and writings of its time. Yet the book has since fallen into disrepute through centuries of scholars who have mistakenly argued that the *Book of Martyrs* is biased and polemical. As Warren W. Wooden ably shows in this first modern survey of Foxe's life and works, the *Acts and Monuments* was a carefully researched and thoroughly documented history of the rise of Protestantism and the excesses of the Counter-Reformation in England. Written by a serious artist who combines the structure of chronicle, allegory, hagiography, and drama, in language that is at once copious and colloquial, the *Acts and Monuments* has as its objectives, according to Wooden, a rewriting of English history and a revelation of the workings of Providence, bringing together plots and personalities, ideas and detailed scenes that would deeply influence generations of English writers, preachers, historians, and artists. The book's ample illustrations, as well as its luxurious printing in large folios, also was meant to emphasize and extend its importance and value. To write his masterpiece, Foxe had to undertake a bold escape from England and, even on his return as a Marian exile under Elizabeth, edit his work carefully. But this man of letters—known for a grammar, for plays, for sermons, and for books of counsel—also had friends in high places, such as John Bale, Nicholas Ridley, and Edmund Grindal, and positions of influence—as tutor to Surrey's children and as a writer patronized by Norfolk—and these helped to make his name a household word in the days of Elizabeth I.

Perhaps because his work is so varied and so extensive, he does not fit categories neatly, and seems hard to see easily and to see whole. The virtue of Wooden's study is that it manages to capture the man and his work with clarity and cogency. As an introductory study, it should prove seminal to students of Foxe specifically but also to all students of Elizabethan literature and culture.

Arthur F. Kinney

Preface

John Foxe is probably the last major Elizabethan author to be rediscovered by the modern age. This unenviable distinction has been previously claimed for such writers as Michael Drayton and Fulke Greville; now, however, in the last quarter of the twentieth century, it is Foxe, an author prolific, talented, and enormously popular with the Renaissance public, whose works have gone out of print and whose name threatens to drop out of Elizabethan literary anthologies and off the syllabuses of academic courses in Renaissance literature. Yet he is the author of one of the most influential and widely read English books ever written. This great book, the *Actes and Monuments of these latter and perillous dayes* . . . (1563) or the *Book of Martyrs,* went through five sixteenth-century editions; and by the ninth edition in 1684 approximately ten thousand copies had been set in circulation in England. According to William Haller, this was "more, it is safe to say, than any other book of similar scope except the Bible." Foxe's popularity during the Renaissance is no less astonishing for its breadth and range, cutting across social divisions and classes to reach all English Protestants with a message that could hardly be more important or timely. Elizabethan authorities made every effort to get the great book into the hands of the public; by canon decree it was set up for public reading in cathedral churches and prominently displayed in the homes of the clergy, while all were enjoined to read it as a civic and religious duty. And like the stage plays of the period, the *Acts and Monuments* spoke also to the nonreading public through the woodcuts which adorned all the Renaissance editions. These were grouped both thematically, as in the sequence illustrating the conflict between papal and monarchical claims of supremacy, and as moving illustrations of particular stories of martyrs; in either case, the message of the pictures, closely coordinated with the text, was the central message of the book, accessible to all who would look. The popularity of the work was further evident in the abridgments, imitations, and off-shoots that sprouted in its wake.

Dramatists drew frequently upon the exciting adventures contained in
Foxe's sprawling history, abridgments began in the Elizabethan era as
an attempt to bring the great book within the price range of ordinary
readers, and the book spawned all sorts of curious progeny such as the
"Joyeous Death" literature for children written by pious Puritan authors like James Janeway and nationalistic attempts to transfer Foxe's
grand design to other countries and other times, as in Cotton Mather's
Magnalia Christi Americani.

Like so many Elizabethan men of letters, Foxe resists narrow literary
labels. His great work, the *Acts and Monuments,* is a central document in
the development of historiography in England. He connects the old
conception of history, as a reflection of the metaphysical struggle
between the forces of Good and Evil, with earthly combatants presented as exemplars of one principle or the other, with a scrupulous
concern for factual data based on the sifting and critical evaluation of
oral testimony and documentary evidence. Thus Foxe is a key transitional figure in the evolution of English historiography. To students of
the Reformation and the development of the Anglican church, Foxe's
works are of paramount importance. Foxe identified the key themes of
the Reformation and hammered them home through the repetition of
illustration after illustration until the most dull-witted reader could not
fail to absorb the pivotal differences between Protestantism and
Catholicism along with the central props for Protestant belief. Foxe also
did much to determine the grounds of the controversy, arguing that
historical fidelity to apostolic principles lay only on the Protestant side
and offering to argue the case through a full-scale appeal to the witness
of history. Thus Foxe helped to shape the controversy along historical
and prophetic lines rather than epistemological or linguistic ones. His
steadfast support of the Anglican church, even when he did not agree in
all points with the Elizabethan Settlement, is also of vital importance to
the development of English Protestantism and the shape of Anglican
belief. Paradoxically, it is probably as a writer, a literary artist, that
Foxe has been most consistently undervalued. Not, to be sure, by the
reading public, which kept his book on the best-seller list from the
sixteenth century to the close of the nineteenth, but by literary critics.
There have been a few recent attempts to cure the critical myopia, most

notably Helen C. White's spirited argument for a reassessment and recognition of Foxe's artistry; but his gifts of expression, character portrayal, and management of narrative sequence are still so little appreciated that even anthologies of English Renaissance literature often either omit him or offer up a page or two of the most horrific stuff a modern editor can select.

Thus, of the three primary areas—historiography, theology, and literature—in which Foxe has a claim on the attention of the modern age, he has been better served by the historians and the theologians than by literary critics. Because of the imbalance, this book, which seeks to survey Foxe's writings and indicate his importance in the three areas, stresses especially his literary artistry, the prose through which his notions of historical theory and religious thought were conveyed to the Renaissance public. Chapter 1 is a brief account of the facts of Foxe's life. The following two chapters focus upon the great work of his lifetime, the *Acts and Monuments,* which he compiled, expanded, and labored over for thirty-five years. Chapter 2 considers the conceptual and ideological structure of the work along with its major themes, noting sources and influences that helped shape the book. Chapter 3 considers the *Acts and Monuments* as a work of literary craftsmanship, examining Foxe's style, narrative stance, biographical strategy, and dramatic power. Chapter 4 surveys Foxe's best minor works, focusing especially upon his contributions to Tudor drama and his achievement as the author of powerful and popular sermons. Chapter 5 returns to the *Acts and Monuments* to trace the curious post-Renaissance publication history of the work, the *Book of Martyrs* as most of its later editors called it, charting its course through the hands of violently partisan editors while seeking to explain why and how the reputation of Foxe and his book, which stood so high for so long, fell into such low estimation. The final chapter considers the current state of Foxe studies and suggests avenues for further exploration.

The appearance of J. F. Mozley's biocritical study of Foxe in 1940 substantially redeemed Foxe's reputation from the tarnish left by over-zealous editors and Victorian detractors. The studies of William Haller in the 1950s and 1960s, culminating in his *The Elect Nation* in 1963, inaugurated a mild stir of interest in Foxe that produced good critical studies by Olsen, White, Yates, and others. I am indebted to the work of these critics as well as to Professors Robert F. Gerke, John J. McKernan, and Joan F. Gilliland who read the manuscript and offered useful suggestions. My research on Foxe has received generous support from several quarters, and I am particularly grateful to the National Endowment for the Humanities for the grant of a Fellowship for Independent Study and Research during 1979–80 which made possible the time to write the book. I am also glad to acknowledge the support of the Marshall University Research Board and the American Philosophical Society for summer grants which facilitated my research on Foxe. Also, I am no less grateful for the consistently sound editorial advice than for the patience of Arthur F. Kinney and the Twayne staff. Finally, I gratefully acknowledge permission granted by the Harvard University Library to reproduce the portrait of John Foxe from Henry Holland's *Herωologia*.

Warren W. Wooden

Marshall University

Chronology

1554 Foxe and wife escape to Continent. September, *Commentarii rerum in ecclesia gestarum* published at Strasbourg.

1555 After his involvement in "the troubles at Frankfort," Foxe moves to Basel, where he works for the Protestant printer, Oporinus, for the duration of his exile.

1555–1558 Aided by material supplied by Edmund Grindal, Foxe works on expanding Latin martyrology to complement English one Grindal's Strasbourg group plans.

1556 *Christus Triumphans.*

1558 Queen Mary dies; Foxe invited to return to England under patronage of his former pupil Thomas, now duke of Norfolk.

1559 August, *Rerum in Ecclesia Gestarum.* Foxe returns to London.

1560 Ordained priest by Edmund Grindal, bishop of London. Son Samuel born.

1563 March 20, *Actes and Monuments. A Brief Exhortation.*

ca. Works for the printer John Daye in London while
1564–1569 gathering material for an expanded edition of the *Actes and Monuments.*

1568 Son Simeon, his father's future biographer, born.

1570 *The Ecclesiastical History. The Sermon of Christ Crucified* delivered at St. Paul's on Good Friday and printed.

1572 Attends the duke of Norfolk at his execution for treason.

1574 Writes Queen Elizabeth and her chief ministers seeking remission of death sentence against two Dutch Anabaptists seized in London.

1576 Another edition of *Acts and Monuments.*

1577 Reply to Portuguese bishop Osorius published.

1578 *A Sermon Preached at the Christening of a Certaine Jew,* delivered the previous year, published in English and Latin editions.

1580   *The Pope Confuted* published in Latin with an English translation the following year.

1583   Last edition of *Acts and Monuments* revised by Foxe. *De Christo Gratis Justificante.*

1587   Foxe dies, April 18; son Samuel has Foxe's commentary on Revelation, the *Eicasmi,* printed.

1596   Last Elizabethan edition of the *Acts and Monuments* containing some additions which may have been prepared by Foxe.

Chapter One

God's Englishman

Early Education, Destitution, and a Miracle

John Foxe was born in the thriving Lincolnshire port city of Boston in 1517, the year Luther posted his theses at Wittenberg signaling the onset of the Reformation. Little is known of Foxe's parents; his son Simeon, in the memoir first prefixed to the eighth edition of the *Acts and Monuments* published in 1641, states that they were "of the Commonalty of that Town, well reputed of, and of good state."[1] His father died while Foxe was quite young, and his mother then married one Richard Melton, whom Foxe thanks (in the dedication of a tract he translated around 1548) for having aided his schooling. Foxe appears to have been a bright and studious youth whose progress in the local grammar school sufficiently impressed his community that several citizens "well approving his good inclination and towardness to Learning" sent him in his sixteenth year to Oxford to continue his studies.[2] He enrolled at Brasenose College where he shared a chamber with Alexander Nowell, the future dean of St. Paul's, ten years Foxe's senior and already attracted to the cause of the reformers. Foxe found Oxford congenial, and in his studies, both at the college and perhaps also at the Magdalen Grammar School, he distinguished himself by his industry and application. He proceeded to the B.A. degree in 1537, followed by the award of a probationary fellowship to Magdalen College in 1538 and election as a Fellow the following year, "a Principal Honour in the University," Simeon notes, since such fellowships, "unless in regard of singular Deserts," were usually reserved for Magdalen men.[3] For the 1539–40 term, Foxe was appointed lecturer in logic; having completed the arts course, he devoted himself especially to studies in divinity. Simeon claims that by the age of twenty-five, his father had "read over all that either the *Greek* or *Latine* Fathers had left in their writings; the Schoolmen in their Disputations; the Councils in their Acts; or the

1

Consistory in their Decrees; and acquired no mean skill in the *Hebrew* Language."[4] In addition to this Scholastic study, Foxe imbibed the humanistic thought and scholarship which had come to characterize Oxford under the patronage of Henry VIII; and it is here that he acquired his lifelong admiration for the work of Erasmus. His course of study at Oxford led in 1545 to the grant of the M.A. degree from Magdalen.

Foxe's conversion to Protestantism occurred during his Oxford years, apparently the product of a slow, agonizing soul-searching rather than the rapturous transport of the Pauline tradition familiar in Puritan conversion narratives. He came to Oxford a Catholic, but he formed friendships with such reformers as Hugh Latimer, John Faulkner, Robert Crowley, and Robert Bertie, as well as Nowell and John Cheke of Cambridge. Still, had there been serious doubts about his orthodoxy as late as 1539, it is unlikely Foxe would have been awarded the Magdalen fellowship. Instead, his studies in ecclesiastical history and observation of the contradiction between the lives and callings of too many men of God led him in time to a period of intense self-analysis luridly described by Simeon:

> By report of some who were Fellow-Students with him, he used over and above his days exercise, to bestow whole nights at his Study, or not till it was very late to betake himself to rest. Near to the Colledge was a Grove, wherein for the pleasantness of the place, the Students took delight to walk, and spend some idle hours for their recreation. This place, and the dead time of the night, had Master *Fox* chosen, with the horror of solitude and darkness, to confirm his mind; which as a fresh-water-Souldier trembled at the guilt of a new imagination.
>
> How many nights he watched in these solitary Walks; what combats and wrastlings he suffered within himself; how many heavy sighs, and sobs, and tears he poured forwith his prayers to Almighty God. . . .[5]

Foxe's irregular hours and unusual conduct were remarked by fellow students and reported to college officials, who monitored his activities for a time. Although it is at least possible that his fellow students and masters were primarily worried about his health, physical and mental, Foxe saw himself as surrounded by a conspiracy of spies, and around September, 1544, he wrote a letter to Dr. Owen Oglethorp, president of Magdalen, defending himself against such charges as inattendance at mass and laughing in church. In the draft letter, he complains that

> My accusers wish to crush me; they strike at my life. I was told a few days ago by a faithful friend, and have since learned by other proofs, that for several months past all my actions have been watched by some of the masters; I cannot move a foot or a finger, but it is observed. They seek to entangle me in the net of their zeal, to endanger my life or fortunes. Have I offended them? Never: but they suspect me to belong to a new religion. Why? Only because they see me study the bible. That is the root. But I am no maker of sects, no lover of strife. . . . I believe in one faith, one truth, one Jesus Christ, one salvation. If I studied scripture, it was to get medicine for my sick soul.[6]

Despite Foxe's fears, no action was taken to dismiss him, and when he resigned his fellowship in 1545, it was apparently a voluntary act, although, as Anthony à Wood noted, he may well have resigned to avoid expulsion.[7] Foxe held strong Protestant views on clerical celibacy, and the Henrician Act of Six Articles—the "whip with six strings" Foxe calls it in the *Acts and Monuments*—which absolutely forbade the marriage of priests was still in force. According to the statutes of Magdalen, every fellow was required to take priest's orders within one year of completing his regency as master of arts. Foxe thus had little choice but to seek employment away from the university. After writing to several friends for assistance in securing a tutorial position, sending a draft of his Latin comedy *Titus et Gesippus* to one as a specimen of his abilities, Foxe was fortunate to learn of a forthcoming vacancy in the household of William Lucy of Charlecote. Following a congenial visit to the household, Foxe accepted the position as tutor to the Lucy children and moved up to Charlecote, where he resided for approximately two years. There on February 3, 1547, Foxe married Agnes Randall of Coventry, apparently also a member of the Lucy household. Later in 1547, still worried about the Six Articles, Foxe determined to leave Charlecote, writing both his stepfather in Boston and his wife's father in Coventry seeking refuge or financial aid. Neither reply was enthusiastic, his stepfather noting that Foxe's suspected heresy might endanger his entire family, and after brief visits to both Coventry and Lincolnshire, Foxe removed to London. There Foxe, who lived all of his adult life on the margin of poverty, sank to a destitution dramatically relieved by "a marvellous accident, and great example of Gods mercy," according to Simeon.[8] One day while Foxe sat on the steps outside St. Paul's, "his countenance thin, and eyes hollow, after the gastful manner of dying-men," a stranger came up to him, pressed a sum of money upon him, and prophesied a very rapid improvement in his circumstances.[9] A few days later, Foxe was offered a position in the household of the duchess of Richmond tutoring the three oldest children of her brother, Henry Howard, the earl of Surrey, recently executed by Henry VIII. Such fortuitous occurrences at crucial points in his life seem to have confirmed Foxe's belief in a special providence and fortified the inner serenity which impressed his contemporaries.

Escape and Exile: *Commentarii rerum in ecclesia gestarum*

Foxe lodged at the duchess's London residence, Mountjoy House, with his charges Thomas, eleven, the future duke of Norfolk, Jane, ten, later countess of Westmoreland, and Henry, eight, afterwards earl of Northampton. In addition to Latin and Greek, Foxe was engaged by the duchess, a favorer of the reformers' cause, to instruct her wards in the Scriptures, and to aid this she gathered at her house such Protestant leaders as John Bale, who became during the summer of 1548 a fast friend of Foxe's. Shortly thereafter, the duchess moved her household to the Reigate manor of her father, the duke of Norfolk, where Foxe found time and opportunity to use his theological and linguistic training. Here he finished English translations of three works by German reformers—Luther, Oecolampadius, and Urban Regius—and published in 1548 *De Non Plectendis Morte Adulteris,* a tract deploring the death penalty for adultery and thereby affording early testimony of his lifelong hatred of capital punishment. As Foxe asks in the tract, "What kind of remedy is it which takes away the life of a sick man?"[10] While his writing career at Reigate was following the familiar pattern of Tudor apprenticeship, Foxe first embarked on his preaching career, helping to establish the reformers' gospel there. In 1550, Foxe was ordained deacon by Nicholas Ridley, bishop of London, and around this time added another pupil to his Reigate charge, young Charles Howard, a Norfolk kinsman who would afterwards achieve lasting fame as Lord

Howard of Effingham, commander of the English forces that repulsed the Spanish armada. An incidental product of this period of teaching was Foxe's *Tables of Grammar,* apparently a textbook on the elements of Latin grammar; the work was not well received and no copies survive. Equally unsuccessful was a tract entitled *De Censura Excommunicatione Ecclesiastica* urging archbishops, bishops, and clergy in positions of authority to revive ecclesiastical excommunication as a means of curbing the corruption and laxity Foxe saw all about him. Although he avers in the *De Censura* that Bishops Latimer and Ridley encouraged him in the composition of the tract, its impact on the clergy was nil.

The social and religious upheaval following the death of Edward VI on July 6, 1553, the short-lived attempt by Northumberland to set Lady Jane Grey and her husband on the throne, and the accession of the eldest child of Henry VIII, the thirty-seven-year-old spinster Queen Mary, came home with a direct, sudden impact to the tutor at Reigate. Among the Roman Catholic prisoners Mary released from the Tower shortly after her coronation were the old duke of Norfolk and Stephen Gardiner, bishop of Winchester. Norfolk sacked Foxe forthwith, sending his grandson Thomas as a page to Bishop Gardiner's household and the other children to similarly reliable Catholic households. An active reformer, a friend and associate of Latimer, Ridley, and Bale, Foxe found his position became daily more precarious, as Mary and Winchester, now her lord chancellor, set about reestablishing Catholicism in England. As the evidence of Mary's papal zeal mounted, Foxe laid plans to go across the seas, but, according to Simeon, he was for a time dissuaded by his former charge Thomas, now seventeen, whom Foxe contrived to visit surreptitiously even within Winchester's house. Simeon's story of Foxe's escape from England is as dramatic and exciting as any of those in the *Acts and Monuments.* One day, while visiting Thomas, Foxe inadvertently entered a room in which Thomas and Winchester were having a conversation. Foxe excused himself immediately, and Winchester, inquiring after him, was told by Thomas that the gentleman was his physician. Winchester's reply, that he liked his face well and would make some use of him, struck Thomas as ominously equivocal; thus he now agreed that Foxe and Agnes, pregnant with their first daughter, must quit the country. Thomas arranged for the Foxes to journey secretly to a rural farm near Ipswich to await the sailing of a ship that one of his servants was dispatched to hire at the port. As soon as the tides were favorable, they embarked at Ipswich into the teeth of a storm so savage that after a day of struggling against it their ship was driven back into the harbor from which they had set sail. There Foxe learned that Winchester's men had located and searched the farmer's house, then proceeded to the docks with a warrant for his arrest, but, learning he had embarked, had left the town. Foxe hired a horse and pretended to ride out of town, returning secretly that evening to persuade the captain of his craft to try once again the crossing. "Whether for reward or pieties sake," the captain agreed and put forth into the rough seas at the turning of the evening tide, conveying Foxe and his wife to Newport within two days.[11] No doubt Foxe, like his son Simeon, reflected upon the "certain course of Providence" which had once more sheltered and sustained him in adversity.[12]

After his arrival on the continent in the spring of 1554, Foxe made his way first to Antwerp, then to Rotterdam on a personal pilgrimage to visit the house in which Erasmus was born, and then to Frankfort where he discussed the great humanist with Froben, Erasmus's Swiss printer, who was attending the Easter book fair. Coming next to Strasbourg, Foxe made arrangements in June with the press of Wende-lin Rihelius to publish a manuscript he had brought with him from England on the martyrs, chiefly English Lollards, of the period 1375–1500. Begun about 1552 and designed to trumpet the history of Wycliffe and the Lollards, little known outside England, and thereby help blunt the Catholic charge that Protestantism was an aberration recently sprung from the spleen of a malcontent German friar, this Latin work was to have traced the resistance to Rome down through the time of Foxe's writing. At Strasbourg, however, Foxe decided to go ahead and publish the first part, down through Savonarola, which appeared as *Commentarii rerum in ecclesia gestarum, maximarumque per totam Europam persecutionum a Wiclevi temporibus ad hanc usque aetatem descriptio* [A commentary on the history of the church, and a description of the great persecutions throughout Europe from the times of Wycliffe to this age], an octavo volume of 212 pages with a dedication dated August 31, 1554. He promised a second part on the persecution of the Lutherans would follow, but it did not. Instead, Foxe moved to Frankfort, the location of a colony of English exiles, where he became embroiled in the internecine controversy known as "the troubles at Frankfort."[13] This bitter controversy centered on the services and prayer book to be used in the Frankfort congregation. In brief, one group within the congregation desired the use of the second, 1552, version of the Book of Common Prayer, while another faction wished a liturgy less conservative than that of the Edwardian prayer book, one more purified. John Knox, who came as preacher to Frankfort from Calvin's Geneva in 1554, was the spokesman for the party of the purified liturgy; Richard Coxe, who had been King Edward's chaplain, led the adherents of the Edwardian prayer book. Although, as J. F. Mozley demonstrates, whenever Foxe appears in this controversy it is on the side of Knox and the radicals,[14] he seems to have tried throughout to act as a mediator and peacemaker between the two factions. Abruptly, early in 1555, the dispute was resolved in favor of Coxe and his party, who outvoted the radicals and then proceeded to inform on Knox to the local authorities, accusing him of treason against the emperor on the basis of some injudicious remarks in one of his tracts. Knox was expelled from the city and, after a rearguard action by members of his faction in the Frankfort congregation, in late summer they too withdrew from Frankfort, Foxe among them. The entire episode at Frankfort, an ominous foreshadowing of subsequent English ecclesiastical controversy, seems to have so soured Foxe on Protestant schism that in later years, despite his differences with elements of the official Anglican order, secession from the established church was never a course he seriously considered.

Foxe journeyed to Basel. There his daughter Christiana was baptized in September, 1555, and he found employment along with his friends John Bale and Lawrence Humphrey as a proofreader for first Froben and then, for the rest of his exile, with the Protestant printer John Oporinus, soon his close friend. While working for the Basel printers, Foxe sought to return to work on the second volume of the *Commentarii* interrupted by his Frankfort sojourn, but several tasks delayed this project. One was work on a translation of Archbishop Cranmer's second book on the Eucharist which replied to Winchester's attack. Peter Martyr, Edmund Grindal, and others had asked Foxe to undertake the English translation; he did, but it proved difficult, both for the technical Latin and the difficulty of checking and correcting citations.

When he finally completed his labors, it apparently proved impossible to find a Swiss publisher willing to print so controversial a book; at any rate, Foxe's translation never appeared in print. Also, from the burning of John Rogers in February, 1555, the reports of the Marian persecution began to travel across the seas, every tide bringing smuggled manuscripts and verbal accounts of the spreading terror. Much of this material passed to Edmund Grindal at Strasbourg who, with other of the exiles there, was collecting documents on the persecution for publication in English. Grindal had no objection to sharing this material with Foxe for his Latin account, and, in fact, he suggested that selected key documents from the persecution might be coordinated and published in English and Latin versions with Foxe's assistance.[15] While he worked at collecting, verifying, and translating this material, Foxe brought out several shorter works from the press of his employer, Oporinus. In March, 1556, appeared *Christus Triumphans,* an "apocalyptic comedy" in Latin verse which Simeon assigns to Foxe's Oxford years. In the fall appeared *Locorum Communium Tituli,* a commonplace book most of whose pages are blank save for headings under which the student was to pen in the appropriate material. In the spring of 1557, Foxe brought out a tract entitled *Ad Inclytos ac Praepotentes Anglia Proceres Supplicatio* appealing to the English nobility to use their influence to stop the Marian persecution.

During this period Foxe sustained himself and his family, which grew in 1558 with the birth of another daughter, Dorcas, through the meager wages he drew from his proofreading and the occasional small sums sent him by such friends as Edmund Grindal. His hopes for patronage from such continental princes as the duke of Würtemberg, to whom Foxe dedicated the *Commentarii* in 1554, had come to nothing, and the years 1557–58 found him living with John Bale and other exiles in an old convent, the Klarakloster, where he continued to sort through the burgeoning records of the Marian persecution. Then came the long-awaited news of the death of Mary on November 17, 1558, and the exiles made haste to return home. Foxe, however, elected to stay on and complete work on his expanded account of the martyrs which was nearly ready for the press. He did add to the torrent of odes, panegyrics, and prayers of welcome to the new queen with a tract entitled *Germaniae ad Angliam Gratulatio* printed by Oporinus in January, 1559. It contained an epilogue to his former pupil Thomas, now duke of Norfolk, who wrote Foxe in May inviting his return and extending his patronage. Meanwhile, as he embarked for England, Grindal wrote Foxe requesting him to delay publication of his book until Grindal and his associates could expand their investigation of the Marian martyrs at first hand for the English martyrology they still hoped to compile as a companion to Foxe's Latin one. No doubt correctly assessing the enormous undertaking of gathering information on the hundreds of people persecuted by the Marian authorities, Foxe instead persevered with his labors, finally bringing out in August, 1559, from the press of Oporinus and Nicholas Brilinger a greatly expanded work entitled *Rerum in Ecclesia gestarum, quae postremis et periculosis his temporibus evenerunt, maximarumque per Europam persecutionum, et sanctorum Dei martyrum, caeterarumque rerum si quae insignioris exempli sint, digesti per regna et nationes commentarii. Pars Prima, in qua primum de rebus per Angliam et Scotiam gestis, atque in primis de horrenda sub Maria nuper regina persecutione narratio continetur* [A commentary of the events that happened in the church in these last perilous times, and mostly of the great persecutions throughout Europe, and of God's holy martyrs, and other notable things, arranged by kingdoms and nations. Part one, containing the narration of the events in England and Scotland, and particularly of the dreadful persecution under Mary, lately queen]. This volume is a folio of 750 pages divided into six books; the first book focuses on the Lollards, incorporating most of the *Commentarii* of 1554; the second deals with the reigns of Henry VIII and Edward VI; and the final four books set forth the Marian persecutions down to the martyrdom of Cranmer on March 21, 1556, with an appended list of the names of those who suffered after that date. Foxe dedicated the work to Norfolk and added a preface on "The Use and Fruits of This History," but the second volume on the continental martyrs promised in the title, like that promised by the 1554 *Commentarii,* never appeared.

Homecoming: *Acts and Monuments*

In October, 1559, having secured financial support to finance his journey, Foxe and his family returned to England to a house in Aldgate furnished him by Norfolk, which served as his chief residence for the next decade. Immediately after his return, Foxe began his long association and close relationship with the great Protestant printer John Daye, who published a small work, Nicholas Ridley's *Friendly Farewell* edited by Foxe, in November, 1559. Over the next fifteen years, Foxe worked closely with Daye, proofreading and editing, sometimes apparently even lodging at his house to be closer to his labors; Daye, in turn, became Foxe's principal publisher and purser.

On January 25, 1560, Foxe was ordained priest in St. Paul's by his friend and fellow exile Edmund Grindal, now bishop of London; but, unlike Grindal, John Almyer, James Pilkington, Alexander Nowell, and other of his fellow exiles who returned to receive important positions in the Elizabethan church, Foxe remained on the fringes of the Anglican establishment, holding only two modest prebends under Elizabeth. One of them, at Shipton, was procured on the queen's instructions for him by William Cecil in 1563 after the great success of the *Acts and Monuments* earlier that year, and Foxe held it until the final year of his life when he passed it on to his son Samuel; the other, at Durham, was procured for him by his old friend James Pilkington, now bishop of Durham, but Foxe resigned it after less than a year, presumably because it was too far from his work in London for regular visits and Foxe had long held strong negative views concerning absentee clerics. But it was most likely his views on the wearing of ecclesiastical vestments which kept him from complying with the usage Elizabeth required of her prominent ecclesiastics that barred his rise within the Anglican establishment.[16] Foxe's modern biographer is probably correct in suggesting that the conversation between Foxe and Archbishop Matthew Parker, preserved in Thomas Fuller's *Church History,* in which Parker seeks unsuccessfully to persuade Foxe to subscribe to the church canons likely alludes to the attempt by the bishops in 1565 to secure uniformity in the wearing of clerical apparel. Certainly Foxe was one of the twenty clerical petitioners of 1564 who sought an indulgence from Parker freeing them from the wearing of vestments. Foxe's exact location on the spectrum of early Elizabethan Protestantism has been a matter of much discussion, with most authorities agreeing that he belonged to the Puritan wing within the Church of England, "an Anglican Puritan," in V. Norskov Olsen's phrase, although some might dissent from Olsen's argument that Foxe was indeed an exemplary figure, "a mirror of Elizabethan Anglican Puritanism."[17] Although not an important officeholder, then, Foxe was nevertheless a popular preacher and evangelist. At the invitation of his friend John Parkhurst, newly consecrated bishop of Norwich, Foxe moved his family to Norwich in 1560, where he seems to have functioned as an evangelist for about a year. His son Samuel was born there on the last day of 1560, and his family continued in residence at Norwich for several years while Foxe returned to his research and writing in London, working toward the English edition of his great book.

Since his return to England, Foxe had been gathering documents, poring over episcopal registers, and interviewing participants in the Marian persecution, and on March 20, 1563, John Daye brought forth from his press the result of Foxe's work, *Actes and Monuments of these latter and perillous dayes, touching matters of the Church wherein ar comprehended and described the great persecutions and horrible troubles that have been wrought and practised by the Romish prelates, specially in this Realme of England and Scotlande, from the yeare of our Lorde a thousande, unto the tyme nowe present. Gathered and collected according to the true copies and wrytinges certificatorie, as wel of the parties them selues that suffered, as also out of the Bishops Registers, which wer the doers therof.* The great folio of almost 1800 pages, three times the size of the 1559 martyrology, was an immediate success; hailed by cleric and layman alike, it immediately established Foxe as one of the leading champions and expositors of the Church of England. In this edition, aimed primarily at his countrymen and so written in English, Foxe expanded his record of the martyrs in the 1559 volume through the addition of much material that had been unavailable to him on the Continent, fleshed out the skeletal list of martyrs from the latter portion of Mary's reign with fuller narratives, added some continental martyrs, and took the history of the church back from Wycliffe to the year 1000, further bolstering the genealogy of anti-Catholic protest, especially in England. Also, the handful of woodcuts of the 1559 edition grew to more than fifty in the English edition, their graphic power a potent supplement to the text; and new prefaces were added: "To the Learned Reader," anticipating the detraction his work would elicit from the contrary party, and "To the persecutors of God's truth, commonly called papists," urging them to read the truth and repent. The edition was dedicated to Queen Elizabeth, one of its chief heroines, and Foxe found himself famous.

The publication of the 1563 folio brought Foxe an outpouring of information from another source, as people from around the country read the stories of their friends and neighbors and wrote or communicated orally to Foxe corrections, addenda, and documents of all kinds for the new edition he must have recognized almost immediately would be necessary. And as Foxe had anticipated, the Roman Catholic campaign against his book began early, with Thomas Harding's slurs on Foxe's "huge dongehill of your stinking martyrs, which ye haue intituled Actes and monumentes"[18] in his tracts against Bishop Jewel in 1565 and 1567, and, more seriously, by the former Marian archdeacon of Canterbury Nicholas Harpsfield in his *Dialogi Sex,* published in Antwerp under the name of Alan Cope in 1566. Foxe considered writing a reply to Harpsfield, but rather than issuing a separate tract he settled on answering his principal charges in the text of the new edition he had begun work on. Meanwhile, Foxe prepared several small works for Daye's press, including his *Syllogisticon,* a compendium of arguments on the eucharistic controversy, *Concio Funebris,* a Latin translation of Grindal's funeral sermon on Emperor Ferdinand, and *A Brief Exhortation* to the Londoners suffering from the outbreak of plague in the summer of 1563. During this period his family expanded with two children, Rafe and Mary, born in early 1565 and his son and future biographer, Simeon, in 1568. The years during the middle and late 1560s appear at a time of intense research and study, of "a most distracted kind of diligence" by Simeon's account,[19] which resulted in the two volume 1570 English edition entitled *The Ecclesiasticall History, Contaynyng the Actes and Monumentes of Thynges passed in euery Kynges tyme in this Realme especially in the Church of England principally to be noted, with a full discourse of such persecutions, horrible troubles, the sufferyng of Martyrs, and other thinges incident, touchyng aswel the sayd Church Of England as also Scotland, and all other foreine nations, from the primitiue tyme till the reigne of K. Henry VIII.* Here Foxe finally worked out the full implications of his vision of ecclesiastical history while carrying the record of the martyrs back to the time of Christ. It is this edition, in 2,300 double-columned folio pages with 150 woodcuts, a new dedication to the queen, and two new addresses, one to reformed Christians, the other to papists, that his modern biographer rightly calls "the crown of his career."[20] This is the edition that the canon law of 1571 directs to be set up in cathedral churches and the homes of various dignitaries of the church along with a copy of the Bishops' Bible.[21]

Following the promulgation of the papal bull excommunicating Queen Elizabeth and the risings in the north, and at the urgent behest of Bishop Grindal, Foxe delivered at Paul's Cross, London, on Good Friday, 1570, his most famous sermon, the *Sermon of Christ Crucified*, published in two editions by Daye in 1570 and in a Latin translation the following year. Next Archbishop Parker requested Foxe's assistance on two projects, one an edition of the proposals for a revised canon law drawn up by Cranmer's commission in the time of Edward VI but never officially adopted, which appeared as *Reformatio Legum Ecclesiasticarum* in 1571, and, in the same year, the other an edition of the Anglo-Saxon gospels with the text of the Bishops' Bible alongside. Also during 1571 Foxe moved from the lodgings provided for him by his patron the duke of Norfolk to a house he purchased in Grub Street, just outside the old city wall. Since serving on the commission of inquiry into the flight of Mary Queen of Scots to England in 1568, Norfolk, whose wife had died the previous year, found himself attracted to the tragic lady and soon enmeshed also in the plots surrounding her, including a scheme supported by Leicester and other nobles for Norfolk to marry the queen. Rumors of the plan reached Foxe, who wrote his former pupil in 1569 warning him of the dangerous course he ran. But Norfolk continued his involvement with Mary until the exposure of the Ridolfi plot, in which he was implicated, following which he was condemned for treason in 1572. Foxe visited him in the Tower and attended him to the scaffold at his execution in June; the duke remembered his tutor with a pension of twenty pounds paid annually for the rest of Foxe's life. The same year Foxe edited the works of the martyrs Tyndale, Frith, and Barnes in one volume, writing biographies of each to accompany the text, which appeared from Daye's press in 1573.

The Final Years: A Living Legend

During the next dozen years, in the wake of the fame assured by the *Acts and Monuments,* Foxe appears as an almost legendary figure, as good Father Foxe, prophet, healer, dispenser of wisdom and charity. Simeon notes that noblemen and Foxe's many friends in the ecclesiastical hierarchy had for years given him sums of money to dispense on charitable causes, and consequently, "no man's house was in those times thronged with more Clients than his. There repaired to him both Citizens and Strangers, Noblemen, and common people of all degrees, and almost all for the same cause; To seek some salve for a wounded conscience. At length, some who were like-wise sick in Body, would needs be carried to him; but this, to stop rumours, he would not suffer to be used. For, because they were brought thither, they were by some reported to be cured."[22] As more Londoners witnessed as well as heard of Foxe's extraordinary devotion to God, Simeon continues, "it so fell out, that they who observed his mind so steadfastly fixed upon God, and that he both spake and did many things beyond the opinion of an ordinary good man, believed that he could not be void of some divine Inspiration; and now some began, not as a good man to honour him, but as one sent from Heaven, even to adore him, through the folly of mankind, madly doting upon any thing. . . ."[23] Thus, ironically, Foxe who had so deplored the creations of Roman Catholic saints' cults was in some danger of becoming himself the object of such a cult. But Foxe's high reputation for piety did have the advantage of giving his words strong moral force, and he spoke out vehemently in 1574 when he wrote the queen, Lord Burleigh, and the Lord Chief Justice trying to obtain remission of the death sentence against two Dutch Anabaptists seized in London, and again in 1581 when he wrote the lords pleading that capital punishment not be inflicted upon Edmund Campion and his fellow conspirators. While his protestations had little effect, his steadfast opposition to capital punishment, whether the victim was a friend or a foe, in an age of intolerance is one of the noblest aspects of his character.[24]

Despite ill health brought on by years of overwork and disregard of his physical needs, Foxe continued his scholarly labors and evangelical works until his death. In 1576, Daye published another edition of the *Acts and Monuments,* very lightly revised. Meanwhile Foxe turned his hand to several controversial works, the first a reply to Osorius, a Portuguese bishop who had written a tract to Queen Elizabeth urging her to return to the Roman Catholic faith. This was published by Daye in 1577 and reprinted in an English translation in 1581. In his *Papa*

Confutatus of 1580, published first in Latin and then in an English translation the same year, Foxe returned to the attack against Rome, and, in 1583, he brought out a work on justification, *De Christo Gratis Justificante,* rebutting Osorius and the Romans. Also during the final decade of his life, Foxe edited and translated various sermons of the continental reformers for several London printers. Foxe's most famous literary work during these years, however, was doubtless his sermon of April 1, 1577, delivered at the public conversion and baptism of Nathanael, a Spanish Jew, in Lombard Street. This was a great public spectacle, and Foxe had had an overflow audience for the event. At the urging of friends, Foxe printed a Latin version as *De Oliva Evangelica Concio* as well as two editions of an English translation entitled *A Sermon Preached at the Christening of a Certaine Jew,* all in 1578. And in 1583 he brought out the fourth edition of the *Acts and Monuments,* reviving the two Latin prefaces of 1563 and the Kalendar of Marytrs, both dropped in 1570 and 1576, and adding a new preface as well as a few additions in the last pages based on records previously unavailable to him. This edition, in two folio volumes of over 2,150 pages, is the final text of the work published in Foxe's lifetime.

The controversial writings of Foxe's final years parallel a period of recurrent turmoil in his private life centered upon his eldest son, Samuel. With the aid of his old friend and fellow exile Lawrence Humphrey, now president of Magdalen College, Foxe managed to procure a fellowship for Samuel there. But he was not the strong student his father had hoped, and paternal apprehension turned to alarm when Samuel abruptly left his studies at Oxford without leave in 1577 and went to France. On Samuel's return, Foxe helped smooth over this peccadillo with the college authorities and all seemed well when Samuel followed his father's path to election as a probationary Fellow of Magdalen in 1579 and a full Fellow the next year. But in 1581 he was expelled from the college, because of the enmity of its powerful Puritan wing. Foxe came again to his son's aid, blasting the Puritan faction and writing influential friends from President Humphrey to Lord Burleigh to have Samuel's fellowship restored, as it was by royal mandate, primarily at the urging of Cecil. Finally, Foxe managed to bestow his prebend at Shipton upon Samuel in 1585. Appropriately, it was Samuel who in 1587 saw through the press the last of his father's writings, a

400-page exposition of the first seventeen chapters of Revelation, entitled *Eicasmi sev Meditationes in Sacram Apocalypsin*. After sending his sons on contrived errands so as to spare them the spectacle of his passing, Foxe died "not through any known Disease, but through much Age," according to Simeon, on April 18, 1587.[25] He was buried in the parish church where he had often preached, St. Giles, Cripplegate, the church of John Speed, Martin Frobisher, Thomas Morley, Lancelot Andrewes, and later John Milton. Simeon records the manner in which the Londoners who had fired their spirits through his works and sought his counsel in times of stress honored his passing: "Upon the report of his death the whole City lamented, honouring the small Funeral which was made for him with the concourse of a great multitude of people, and in no other fashion of mourning than as if among so many, each man had buried his own Father, or his own Brother."[26]

Chapter Two

The *Acts and Monuments:* The Grand Design

Although in a lifetime of writing and editing he published a number of tracts, sermons, treatises, and translations, Foxe is remembered today almost exclusively as the author of *The Book of Martyrs,* as the *Acts and Monuments* has been popularly called ever since the publication of the first English edition in 1563. The estimate of history is in; for centuries he has been John Foxe the Martyrologist, preeminently the author of one of the most influential English books ever written. The *Acts and Monuments* as it appears today, reprinted in our time from the last Victorian edition in eight bulky and unattractive volumes of 6,000 pages, is far different from the little martyrology Foxe set out to prepare in the opening years of the 1550s. In the metamorphosis from a little Latin octavo to a massive multivolume work containing thousands of pages of stirring English prose, a clear controlling design emerged, an amalgam of Foxe's study of classical and contemporary authors and his intensive study of the Bible to convey the message of the martyrs and their church to an eager public.

The Intellectual Context

In the early 1550s, Foxe had a relatively comfortable situation in comparison with the penury in which he often lived, with a tutorial position at Reigate which allowed sufficient free time to pursue his scholarly and evangelical interests. Simeon notes that while at Oxford his father had made a special study of ecclesiastical history, an area of acute concern for reformers. By breaking away from the Roman Catholic church, the sole visible and continuous church of Christ through history, the reformers opened themselves to the contemptuous question

17

put by inquisitor after inquisitor in the *Acts and Monuments:* "Where was your church thirty years ago?" A partial answer to this query was to invoke the pre-Reformation opposition to Rome, especially those who had given their lives in resistance to the papacy and its claims, as evidence of a continuous history of opposition to abuses and corrupt innovations within the Roman Catholic church. In surveying this ground, Foxe fixed in particular on John Wycliffe and his followers, the Lollards, who arose in fourteenth-century England to defy Roman authority. Then in 1548 at the home of the duchess of Richmond, Foxe met John Bale, the former Carmelite monk turned skilled Protestant propagandist, who was already excavating this ground with *A brefe Chronycle concernynge the Examinacyon and death of the blessed martyr of Christ Syr Johan Oldecastell* (1544), which laid the groundwork for the development of a Protestant hagiography.[1] Bale followed in 1546 with *The first Examination of Anne Askewe,* a martyr of the 1530s whose story Foxe incorporated in the *Acts and Monuments* from Bale's account; thus the spiritual heritage of the reformers, from Lollard to Tudor, was established, waiting only for a chronicler to research and fill in the figures in the anti-Roman tradition. This Foxe set out to do in the early 1550s, apparently envisioning a volume on the Lollard martyrs and their heirs down to the great watershed of Luther, whose story would be followed by an account of the Tudor martyrs through the Henrician period.

When Foxe escaped from England in 1554, he must have carried with him a manuscript containing the first portion of his project, for at the end of the summer of 1554 he brought out a Latin octavo entitled *Commentarii. . . .* This small volume covered the period of approximately 1375–1500, concentrating on the English Lollards. This Lollard martyrology Foxe intended to bring up to the present, but he was prevented by other pressing duties, including his translation of Cranmer's book of the Eucharist, his summons to Frankfort and preaching duties there, and the terrible news from England that under Mary the fires of Smithfield were being rekindled, claiming their first victim, John Rogers, in February, 1555. Soon after, the transcripts, eyewitness accounts, letters, and other documents of the Marian martyrs began to flow from England to the Continent, usually passing first through the hands of Grindal at Strasbourg, whose group labored on their vernacular account of the persecution, then on to Foxe for his expanded Latin volume. This publication, which appeared as *Rerum in Ecclesia Gestarum . . .* in 1559, reproduced the *Commentarii* of 1554 as its first book, then included another covering the reigns of Henry VIII and Edward VI, and four books on the Marian martyrs, the whole bound up in a 750-page folio. While this volume more closely answered Foxe's original intent in setting out to write a martyrology, the 1559 book was deficient in that the records of recent persecutions which had reached Foxe were too incomplete and fragmentary to fashion into a narrative of the years just past. The *Rerum in Ecclesia Gestarum* thus ends with an account of the martyrdom of Cranmer on March 21, 1556, followed by a list on the last four pages of names of those who had suffered under Mary subsequent to Cranmer's burning.

Upon his return to England in 1559, Foxe finally had direct access to the primary materials needed to correct and fill out his account of the Marian martyrs and to complete the record left unfinished in the *Rerum in Ecclesia Gestarum* volume. He examined as many registers as he could in London and the surrounding southeastern region where the persecution had been most severe, interviewed survivors and witnesses, and engaged in a voluminous correspondence, much swollen after the publication of the first English edition, with people all over England who had some story or detail to contribute to the history of the martyrs. Apparently during this period Grindal, who at the time of his return still hoped to publish an English account of the martyrs, turned over the martyrs' records his group had collected to Foxe. As inheritor of the Grindal project, and prompted by his own patriotism and sense of England's preeminence in the history of the true church and resistance to the false, Foxe elected to print the third version of his work in the English vernacular which, he explained in his preface "The Utility of This Story," "as I have taken in hand chiefly for the use of the English church, so have I framed it in that tongue which the simple people could best understand."[2] The edition of 1563, the *Actes and Monuments,* created a sensation and, despite its bulk, became a best-seller. It made its author famous although not wealthy, since he received no royalties from its sale.

The Making of the Grand Design

The *Acts and Monuments* represents a significant development on the early versions of Foxe's martyrology, not only because it is in the vernacular and at 1,800 folio pages more than twice the size of its 1559 predecessor, but especially because it refines Foxe's purpose and design. In this edition, the martyrology of the Latin versions is on the way to becoming something different and, eventually, more important: an ecclesiastical history of the church of Christ to the time of Foxe's writing. Along with all the new information on the Marian martyrs, Foxe now extends his coverage back to approximately the year 1000 A.D., a time, he explains, when Satan broke loose from the millenial bondage prophesied in the book of Revelation, and consequently an era which marked a crucial turning point in the history of the church. Thus, Foxe continues, although the Roman Catholic church had often erred in the early period up to "the 1000 yeares after Christe, yet in respect of the other time that followed, it might seme a golden age full of much light, vertue, and true felicitie"[3]; and it is immediately clear that he intends a survey of increasing ecclesiastical corruption within the visible church, for "to geue thee one generall rule for all, this thou shalt observe, the higher thou goest upwarde to the Apostles time, the purer thou shalt finde the churche: the lower thou doest descend, euer the more drosse and dregges thou shalt perceyue in the bottome, and especiallye within the laste 500 yeares."[4] This Pauline conception of the apostolic church as pure font was probably impressed upon Foxe by his close study of *The Ecclesiastical History* of Eusebius of Caesarea, the third-century bishop whose work is one of Foxe's primary models and, in the 1570 *Acts and Monuments,* one of his sources. But Foxe is far more schematic than Eusebius. Within the history so starkly divided by the year 1000 into pure and corrupt, he further subdivides the history of the church into five eras: the birth and infancy in the time of Christ; the spread of the gospels by the apostles throughout the Roman empire; the flourishing age when the church grew through persecution until the Christianization of the empire under Constantine; the middle age when "she wrastled with sondrie sectes, schismes, and schismatickes" ending with the period of decay turning into rampant corruption; and finally the period of Foxe's narration, "the time, that the reuelation speaketh of, when Sathanas, the old serpent, beyng tied up for a thousand yere, was losed for a certaine space, of ye which space, here in thse bokes . . . we entend some thing to entreat and speake of."[5]

The four periods of the early church only enumerated here Foxe fills out in the 1570 edition, but as early as the 1563 edition the martyrology is augmented by a history of the church through the Middle Ages to the Tudors in which the imperial theme, as Frances Yates calls it, is a prominent new feature.[6] Much chronicled material is added on the development of the English church especially during the medieval period, material which Foxe arranged and organized about the struggle of sovereign emperors on the Continent as in England to resist the machinations and boundless greed of a newly militant papacy. Thus, as early as 1563, Foxe develops a dual focus, and with the publication in 1570 of the two-volume edition, which takes the history of the church and the martyrs back to the time of Christ, the twin themes of the histories of martyrs and emperors opposing the papacy dominate. With his emphasis on the antiphonal opposition of godly monarchs and saintly martyrs to a corrupt visible church presided over by a power-mad papacy, Foxe brought his grand design to its final form. Now, he writes proudly in one of the new prefaces which replaced most of those in the earlier English edition, through his history he has restored to the reformers their heritage, the true heritage of Christ's apostolic church, "which persecuted church, though it hath been of long season trodden under foot by enemies, neglected in the world, not regarded in histories, and almost scarce visible or known to worldly eyes, yet it hath been the true church only of God, wherein he hath continually wrought hitherto, in preserving the same in all extreme distresses, continually stirring up from time to time faithful ministers, by whom always have been kept some sparks of his true doctrine and religion" (1:xix). In 1570, Foxe's great work was substantially complete, his design intact and finished; the two subsequent editions in Foxe's lifetime, in 1576 and 1583, added only a little additional material, chiefly some continental stories of martyrs for the post-Marian period.

The Use of Historical Sources

The fact that Foxe wrote his narratives of martyrs and monarchs in conflict with an institutional religion he clearly regarded as degenerate has long proved a barrier to an accurate estimate of his achievement as an historian. Does the controlling apocalyptic design of the whole and the undisguised partisanship of the author vitiate any claim his work might have as a serious history? From the Victorian attacks of S. R. Maitland until the landmark study by J. F. Mozley in 1940, most scholars rated Foxe high as a propagandist but either denied or ignored his positive contribution to historiography. As William Lamont observed a decade ago, it is only very recently that Foxe's reputation has advanced "beyond that of a teller of Papist atrocities to credulous bigots."[7] For some critics still, Foxe's book is yet no more than a monument to prejudice, a work credulous, uncritical, and imaginative on Philip Hughes's examination.[8] But despite an almost medieval controlling design and an embarrassingly frank bias in the work, many modern scholars have come to concede that Foxe's respect for documentation and habit of including primary sources in his text marks a significant advance in the development of English historiography.[9]

The important point in this reevaluation is that neither Foxe's partisanship nor his commitment to a grand ideological design were permitted to override his respect for the integrity of his sources, the wealth of printed and manuscript material he reproduces verbatim in the *Acts and Monuments*. Where Foxe depends on earlier historians, he is far more scrupulous than the habits of his age required about citing his guides, usually chapter and verse. When his sources conflict, as in the casualty statistics for the Battle of Barnett during the Wars of the Roses where Polydore Vergil counts 10,000 slain but Robert Fabian numbers only 1,500, Foxe records both estimates along with some pointed comments on the unreliability of chronicles (3:750). Even when Foxe came across a story entirely congruent with his ideological design, as in the story of King John's death from poison administered by a monk, he did not embrace it uncritically if alternate accounts were on record. Considering Foxe's religious bias and the general conception of history in the sixteenth century, F. J. Levy singles out the mode of King John's death as evidence of Foxe's practice of insisting on clear and convincing factual evidence in a manner altogether remarkable for his age: "Foxe would have liked to believe the story since it fitted so well with his bias. It turned out, however, that the chronicles were not in agreement on the point, and Foxe, as befitted an honest man, quoted alternative accounts. In the end, he accepted the poisoning story, but it was not without some sifting of the evidence."[10]

Of course, Foxe was at the mercy of his evidence, and up until his death he continued collecting materials for the *Acts and Monuments,* calling all along on his readers to aid him with any information they might possess.[11] And he was not free of the typical Renaissance historical habits discounted by the modern age; for example, in the absence of accurate records, Foxe occasionally adopts the manner of Polydore Vergil, Thomas More, and other contemporary historians in inventing speeches for his characters, as in his account of Winchester's attempt to discredit Queen Catherine Parr in the eyes of Henry VIII. Also in sections such as that entitled "The Severe Punishment of God Upon the Persecutors of His People and Enemies to His Word . . .," while he cites authorities for his grisly anecdotes, Foxe was surely unwise to accept some of the more improbable of the stories. On the whole, however, Levy is correct in his assertation that Foxe's "skepticism was pervasive"; indeed, Foxe's own procedures as he describes them compare favorably with modern ones:

diligence is required, and great searching out of books and authors, not only of our time, but of all ages. And especially where matters of religion are touched pertaining to the church, it is not sufficient to see what 'Fabian' or what 'Hall' saith; but the records must be sought, the registers must be turned over, letters also and ancient instruments ought to be perused, and authors with the same compared: finally, the writers amongst themselves are to be conferred one with another; and so with judgment matters are to be weighed; with diligence to be laboured; and with simplicity, pure from all addition and partiality, to be uttered. (3:376–77)

This respect for documentary evidence and the accurate reproduction of primary texts and sources is something new for mid-Tudor England. Even when there is obviously material missing from a vital document, Foxe refrains from filling out the missing pages with conjectural reconstruction and simply notes the fact of the lacuna; similarly, he resists the urge to revise the account of hostile authorities, contenting himself with noting for the reader the origin and bias of a given witness or document. This treatment of documents is a testimony to the editorial example of Erasmus in particular and the humanist historiographers in general upon Foxe. Thus, as Paul Christianson observes, Foxe adopts humanist learning and techniques of history writing "to the production of books meant for the common man as well as the scholar," including along with his text and interpretation as much of his documentary source material as it was feasible to print.[12] On this view, the *Acts and Monuments* "stood in the mainstream of the new learning,"[13] evidence, in the words of another recent critic, that Foxe's "command of documentary and reported detail is unapproached by anything else that has come down from the same period."[14] Modern historians who have tried to retrace the evidence for sections of his history give him good marks for accuracy;[15] but no less important, despite the controlling design of the work, Foxe is acquitted of the old charge of tampering with evidence to support his thesis. John T. McNeill's conclusions on this score are widely shared by modern scholars and contribute significantly to the postwar "rebunking," in Gordon Rupp's fine phrase,[16] of Foxe's reputation as an historian: "We may say, I think, that he never allows it [his apocalyptic design] to determine the dates or sequences of events furnished through documented sources."[17] Hence the *Acts and Monuments* affords the paradoxical combination of an anachronistically modern and realistic foreground within a mythic controlling framework.

Theological Currents and Cosmic Design

Few of the ingredients of Foxe's grand design were original with him; his genius lay rather in his enormous devotion to the project and capacity for work (in a word, his zeal), his power of synthesis, and his extraordinary narrative gifts. "His greatness is that many were his mentors but he was the disciple of none," V. Norskov Olsen argues in his monograph on Foxe's ecclesiological thought.[18] Of course, the key guide for Foxe, as for all reformers, was the sacred scriptures, the authentic word of God. His particular fascination was with the prophetic books of Daniel and St. John, wherein he was sure God had revealed through dark figures His divine plan for human history, disclosing the course of His true church and people down to the end of time. Foxe's friend John Bale had mined the field extensively in his commentary on that Apocalypse entitled *The Image of Bothe Churches* (1545), and in 1563 Foxe had followed Bale and most other expositors in dating the binding of Satan forecast in Revelation from the time of Christ's resurrection to 1000 A.D., coinciding with an increase in papal militancy under Pope

Sylvester II. At this time Satan is loosed, preparing the way for Antichrist and leading after several centuries to the struggle of the reformers against him and the final conflict between Christ and Antichrist, the true church and the false.

There were problems here, however. As Foxe recalls in a vivid passage in the 1570 *Acts and Monuments,* this schematization worried him, for it placed the terrible persecutions of the Roman emperors during a time when Satan was bound, leading the martyrologist himself to question God's doings. The solution to this dilemma came to him early one sleepless Sunday morning as he lay in bed revolving the problem in his mind: he had misinterpreted the numerology of Revelation. By reinterpreting the mystical numbers, Foxe discovered that the correct chronology of the thousand-year binding of Satan dated not from the time of Christ's resurrection but from the year 324 A.D., with the close of the Roman persecution and the Christianization of the empire by Constantine, son of a Briton mother and commander of British legions.[19] This new and unique interpretation of the millenium had the great advantage of placing the unleashing of Satan and the resistance it provoked among true Christians early in the fourteenth century, just at the time Foxe's countryman, John Wycliffe, arose to spark a reform movement, a man, as John Alymer wrote in 1559, whom England had not sufficiently recognized and honored, "that servant of Christ John Wyclif, who begat Hus, who begat Luther, who begat the truth."[20] Also with this new dating, Antichrist begins to stir during the period the recently established order of friars ("the body of Antichrist" Foxe calls them) fanned out from Italy spreading mischief, while on the other side, the friends of truth welcomed at the same time the composition of Marsilius of Padua's *Defensor Pacis,* perhaps the most comprehensive medieval attack on the papacy's claims to temporal power. Thus, with Constantine bringing peace to the church at one end of the millenial period and Wycliffe raising the cry of reform on the other, Britain's place in the history of the true church became a crucial one—and the foundation for an interpretation of England's role as God's "elect nation," in William Haller's phrase, was established.[21]

Foxe read extensively in the literature of church history, from his study of the church fathers at Oxford through his reading in the histories and chronicles written in the sixteenth century, and scholars point to several prominent early authors as important secondary influences upon the martyrologist. In his own time Foxe was called the Elizabethan Eusebius, and in the dedication to Queen Elizabeth of the 1563 edition, Foxe explicitly compares himself to Eusebius and the queen to Constantine, the emperor to whom Eusebius presented his *Ecclesiastical History*. Foxe relies heavily upon this history for his own account of the early persecutions throughout the Roman Empire, and both Eusebius' stress on a fugitive church made up of a small band of the faithful keeping the gospel word alive and his reiterative demonstration of the working of divine reward and, especially, retribution are concepts mirrored throughout the *Acts and Monuments*. Also from Foxe's study of the church fathers during the classical period, the thought of St. Augustine contributed to his conception of the development of the church through history. Although he did not adhere strictly to Augustine's periodization of history, the polarization between the City of God and that of the World spoke directly to Foxe's stark view of a grand division preordained by God of all mankind into the elect and the reprobate, the two locked in conflict until the end of time. And Augustine's division was, as D. M. Loades observes, "a distinction which cut across the visible divisions of the church and secular society," thereby minimizing the importance of an institutional church liable to corruption and exalting the spiritual community of the faithful, the invisible church.[22]

Among Foxe's contemporaries, William Tyndale, one of the pioneer English Protestant historians and a famous martyr whose story is told in great detail in the *Acts and Monuments,* through his *Practice of Prelates* and other works both contributed the identification of Antichrist through the ages with the papacy and set the pattern for interpreting the ecclesiastical history of England in the Middle Ages as "an international conspiracy led by Antichrist disguised as the Pope, seeking to make the English kings their submissive servants."[23] Throughout this period God sent His prophets such as Wycliffe to warn of the menace, but in the struggle between the elect and the persecuting church, the former would suffer horribly before the final victory. Among continental historians, Matthias Flacius of Illyria is frequently considered an important contributor to the development of Foxe's conception of ecclesiastical history. Foxe was working for Oporinus as proofreader in

1556 when Flacius's collection of martyrs' histories appeared from that press as *Catalogus Testium Veritatis.* More important for the *Acts and Monuments,* however, is the massive *Ecclesiasticae Historiae* or "Madeburg Centuries" edited by Flacius and published in thirteen volumes in Basel from 1561–74. Here are worked out many of the ideas Foxe applied to his tracing of English ecclesiastical history, in particular the cosmic conflict of Christ and Antichrist in terms of the elect versus the papacy and the preservation and continuity of the true gospel through the noninstitutional church of the elect, whom God intervenes to protect and nurture through the course of history. Finally, Johannes Sleidan's history of the Reformation under Charles V, which appeared in 1555 with an English translation in 1560, employs the familiar apocalyptic framework and periodization of church history and was known to Foxe.

The Philosophical Eusebius

From among these various influences on Foxe's ecclesiological and historical thought, modern commentators increasingly single out as paramount Foxe's friend, fellow exile, and co-worker, John Bale, the fiery Protestant propagandist. As a Protestant hagiographer and a leading expositor of apocalyptic thought in his printed works, Bale's influence on Foxe has been noted already, but the consanguinity between the two men fostered by the period at Basel when they worked side by side proofreading and editing Protestant texts while both lodged at the Klarakloster may well suggest an influence deeper than the evidence of Foxe's borrowings from Bale's printed works. The possibility that Bale also may have served as a conduit and interpreter of popular theories of ecclesiastical historiography is suggested by Olsen, while Paul Christianson points to Bale's reworking of ancient and modern views of the history of the church as the prototype, if not actually the model, for Foxe's: "Bale took St. Augustine's idea of the two cities and transformed it into that of two churches—one headed by Christ and the other by antichrist. He thereby institutionalized Tyndale's designation of antichrist as the representative of evil on earth through all ages. A differentiation of this type solved one of the key problems of the reformation—the tracing of legitimate authority, a problem faced by protestants especially, for they could not rely on an unbroken institutional tradition for their defence. By applying the idea of the two churches, Bale stood history on its head."[24] This inversion of history, with the visible, Roman Catholic church fallen into decay and corruption while the true church becomes a spiritual one maintained by persecuted fugitives, contains the outline of Foxe's view of ecclesiastical history wherein Protestant doctrine is found to be the ancient truth and Roman Catholicism the novelty.

As ecclesiastical historian, then, Foxe applies an apocalyptic time scheme derived from his study of the Bible to the history of the church, explaining its flourishing periods and subsequent decay down to his own day, when the partisans of Antichrist and those of the true gospel drew up their ranks for the final conflict at the end of time which Foxe, like most reformers, felt to be near at hand. His periodization of history, his apocalyptically based time schemes, was sufficiently clear and, to sixteenth-century Protestants, convincing that there is justice in William Lamont's claim that despite the various apocalyptic theorists of the era, it is Foxe who "made the pursuit of the Millenium respectible and orthodox . . . who domesticated the Apocalypse."[25] Beyond the grand conflict of the two cities, of God and the World, Foxe distinguishes the city of God as manifested institutionally in the church of God as composed of two factions, the true and the false Christians, as in his description of the visible church:

The world, I call all such as be without or against Christ, either by ignorance not knowing him, or by heathenish life not following him, or by violence resisting him. On the other side, the kingdom of Christ in this world, I take to be all them which belong to the faith of Christ, and here take his part in this world against the world; the number of whom although it be much smaller than the other, and always, lightly, is hated and molested of the world, yet it is the number which the Lord peculiarly doth bless and prosper, and ever will. And this number of Christ's subjects is it, which we call the visible church here in earth; which visible church, having in itself a difference of two sorts of people, so is it to be divided into two parts, of which the one standeth of such as be of outward profession only, the other of such as by election inwardly are joined to Christ: the first in words and lips seem to honour Christ, and are in the visible church only, but not in the church invisible, and partake the outward sacraments of Christ, but not the inward blessing of Christ. The other are both in the visible, and also in the invisible church of Christ, which not in words only and outward profession, but also in heart do truly serve and honour Christ, partaking not only the sacraments, but also the heavenly blessings and grace of Christ.

And many times it happeneth, that as between the world and the kingdom of Christ there is a continual repugnance, so between these two parts of this visible church aforesaid ofttimes groweth great variance and mortal persecution, insomuch that sometimes the true church of Christ hath no greater enemies than those of their own profession and company; as happened not only in the time of Christ and his apostles, but also from time to time almost ever since; but especially in these latter days of the church under the persecution of Antichrist and his retinue; as by the reading of these volumes more manifestly hereafter may appear. (1:88)

As the members of only the visible church unite with the agents of the World, pagans from Roman magistrates to Turks, in persecution of the members of Christ's true, invisible church, the prophecies of Revelation—of the unleashing of Satan, of the rise of Antichrist, of the whore of Babylon come to copulate with the kings of the world—all for Foxe are confirmed in history. These members of the invisible church from which the ranks of the martyrs are filled down through history constitute the link between the apostles and the reformers celebrated in the two Latin martyrologies Foxe published in the 1550s. Theirs is the true tradition, and the martyrs are one of the strongest proofs of their faith. Thus, once the martyr stories are interwoven into the overarching apocalyptic framework, the result, as William Haller observes, is that "history was authenticated by prophecy and prophecy was confirmed by history."[26]

The framework is a solid one; Foxe's text belies the early impression it may give of a disordered jumble. The design of the *Acts and Monuments* from 1570 on divided the work into twelve books encompassing the five periods of the church and covering its establishment, rise, decay, and reformation. Set in the context of an historical narrative offering a convincing justification and rationale for their suffering, the stories of martyrs were now part of a coherent philosophical view of history in a volume swollen by the inclusion of documents of all sorts that bolstered both aspects of Foxe's story and gave the work a massive solidarity which daunted even his enemies. Helen C. White admirably describes the effect of this end product of Foxe's long labors: "There can have been few books in the world like it, few that would give an innocent reader such a sense of being in the know, past, present, and future, that would give a simple man so complete a picture of the world in which he found himself and how it came to be so; few books that would so completely furnish forth an untutored mind with a whole intellectual world, so perfectly suited to its tastes and adapted to its powers, so completely to arm it against the challenges and pressures of an age of unprecedented moral and mental aggression."[27]

Themes: The Nature and Value of Martyrdom

Several fundamental themes in Foxe's thought prominent in the "whole intellectual world" he offers the reader of the *Acts and Monuments* warrant individual attention. The first is Foxe's conception of the nature, value, and historical importance of the martyrs whose stories he relates. When Nicholas Harpsfield attacked him for naming as martyrs people like John Wycliffe, who died peacefully in his own bed, Foxe replied that such were "faithful witnesses of Christ's truth and testament," and, noting the word in Greek means "witness-bearer," he defended his usage as appropriate for those who stood for Christ even without having to pay the extreme penalty (3:53n.). In this case, the term could be stretched, for example, to fit Elizabeth, who as princess during her sister's reign was imprisoned in the Tower, examined for evidence of complicity in Wyatt's rebellion, and considered suspect throughout on account of her Protestantism. It was this desire to witness for Christ's truth that drove even ordinary men and women to unsuspected heights of heroism, or fanaticism depending on one's point of view, compelling them to forsake their own safety to speak out against Romish error and for the gospel truth. In fact, these faithful witnesses so frequently eschew their own safety and security in the *Acts and Monuments* that the reader may register pride or sadness but not surprise when he comes to a story such as that of the bright young gospeller John Frith, who in the time of Henry VIII was arrested, examined, and conveyed under guard by the bishop of Cambridge's men to Croydon where he was to be condemned and burned as a heretic. On the journey his steadfast faith and humble demeanor so impressed his jailers that they proposed he take a horse and escape across the fields while they covered for him. To this kind offer Frith replied that "if I should now start aside and run away, I should run from my God, and from the testimony of his holy word, worthy then of a thousand hells. And therefore I most heartily thank you both, for your good wills towards me, beseeching you to bring me where I was appointed to be brought; for else I will go thither all alone" (8:699).

These faithful witnesses, most of whom did suffer unto death, in fact form the core of the *Acts and Monuments,* even after the addition of the grand design and historical panoply of the ecclesiastical history. Thus, although Foxe is quite correct in pointing out to Harpsfield that "I wrote no such book bearing the title of the 'Book of Martyrs'" (3:392), it is not a title he disdains. For the populace had adopted and popularized the ersatz title and, however much modern critics deplore Foxe the martyrologist overshadowing Foxe the ecclesiastical historian, it is the martyrdoms, the physical witness in combination with the spiritual one, that are the emotional center and the key to the popularity of the work. In an age of confusion, change, and uncertainty, when even the godly like Thomas Cranmer might find themselves driven to recanting recantations, what was needed was the example of the firm anchor represented by the martyrs holding steadfast amid the pitch and tumult of the times. The ultimate testimony of faith then is not words alone, especially against an enemy adept at sophistry, but words sealed by acts, preeminently the supreme act of witnessing for the true faith to the death, and thus imitating the sacrifice of the Cross. These acts are the compulsion that led Foxe to write his great work, for in the preface, "The Utility of This Story," he recalls that "when I weighed with myself what memorable acts and famous doings this latter age of the church hath ministered unto us by the patient sufferings of the worthy martyrs, I thought it not to be neglected, that so precious monuments of so many matters, meet to be recorded and registered in books, should lie buried by my default, under darkness of oblivion" (1:xxv). Their stories constitute a precious treasure, for "by reading thereof we may learn a lively testimony of God's mighty working in the life of man, contrary to the opinion of Atheists, and all the whole nest of Epicures" (1:xxv). Thus, even for those who live in quieter times, the inspiration and the model of the martyrs endures, for, as Foxe exhorts the reader of the *Acts and Monuments*, "if their blessedness be most certain and sure, then let us direct the course of our life to the same felicity. These men have forsaken this life, yet let us not be slow to correct and amend the same; and though we cannot die with them in like martyrdom, yet let us mortify the worldy and prophane affections of the flesh, which strive against the spirit" (6:276).

On several occasions Foxe quotes approvingly the dictum of Tertullian that "the blood of martyrs is the seed of the gospel," nourishing and glorifying the church.[28] For their example so astonishes the worldly that it attracts adherents to study, appreciate, and believe the cause for which the martyrs sacrifice themselves. Hence the paradox Foxe borrows from Tertullian that "this sect will never die, which, the more it is cut down, the more it groweth" (1:159). While their reward is heavenly, the martyrs' example both produces immediate beneficial results by winning the hearts, minds, and souls of those who see or read of the martyrs' witness and also keeps alive the pure tradition of the apostolic church. Foxe's book is replete with examples, from Roman soldiers to Tudor tradesmen, won to Christ through the example of the martyrs. Thus Julius Palmer, a resolute Oxford papist, began by mocking the martyrs, saying "that none of them all would stand to the death for their religion" (8:206). But he was so moved by hearing a firsthand account of the horrible death of Bishop Hooper that he attended the examination and execution of the Oxford martyrs, Ridley and Latimer, "at what time, in the hearing of divers of his friends, he brast out into these words and such like: 'O raging cruelty! O tyranny tragical, and more than barbarous!'" (8:206). The spectacle of the bishops' godly parting proves the catalyst for Palmer's conversion; he joins the reformers and, in due course, is himself persecuted and finally martyred for the same faith. The example of these Tudor martyrs in particular was so potent that, according to Foxe, instead of deterring others from embracing their cause, the original intent of the persecutions, their suffering evoked a widespread public sympathy even when souls such as Palmer's were not won as a direct result. As early as the Henrician persecutions, Foxe records such stories as that of the death of one Kerby, a simple Suffolk husbandman, which illustrate the point. At this execution, Foxe writes,

Kerby, taking his nightcap from his head, put it under his arm, as though it should have done him service again; but, remembering himself, he cast it from him, and lifting up his hands, he said the hymn Te Deum, and the Belief, with other prayers in the English tongue. The lord Wentworth, while Kerby was thus doing, did shroud himself behind one of the posts of the gallery, and wept, and so did many others. . . . Then fire was set to the wood, and with a loud voice he called unto God, knocking on his breast, and holding up his hands, so long as his remembrance would serve, and so ended his life; the people giving shouts, and praising God with great admiration of his constancy, being so simple and unlettered. (5:532)

By the time of the full rage of the Marian persecutions popular sympathy for the victims was much increased. Thus Foxe records such examples of popular resistance to the official examiners and support for the persecuted reformers as the embarrassing problem for the tormentors occasioned by the communal sympathy for Walter Mille, martyred in 1558: "Yea, the whole town was so offended with his unjust condemnation, that the bishop's servants could not get for their money so much as one cord to tie him to the stake, or a tarbarrel to burn him; but were constrained to cut the cords of their master's own pavilion, to serve their turn" (5:646).

Each martyr is then an individual witness while collectively they keep alive the traditions and beliefs of the church of the elect, for persecution is one of the marks of the elect; thus, as one of Wycliffe's followers affirms, "whomsoever the Lord vouchsafeth to receive to be his children, those he scourgeth: for so the merciful Father will have them tried in this miserable life by persecutions, that afterwards he may spare them" (3:506). Persecution is one of the ways God affirms and makes known His true church to all men; commenting on the time of trial initiated by the Marian persecution, John Bradford, one of the most eloquent of the Tudor martyrs, writes that "Now will God make known his children. When the wind doth not blow, then cannot a man know the wheat from the chaff; but when the blast cometh, then flieth away the chaff, but the wheat remaineth, and is so far from being hurt, that by the wind it is more cleansed from the chaff, and known to be wheat. Gold, when it is cast into the fire, is the more precious: so are God's children by the cross of affliction. Always God beginneth his

judgment at his house" (7:197). Further, the suffering of these true
witnesses works to draw the church back to its fundamental principles
and beliefs, both too easily obscured in sectarian squabbling during
peaceful times. But most important of all, the martyrs are keys in the
history of God's church and constitute an unbroken phalanx of witnesses to its faith and principles stretching from the Tudor fires of
Smithfield back to the savage arenas and crucifixions of the pagan
Roman Empire. As in the Kalendar of Martyrs Foxe prefixed to the
1563 edition of the *Acts and Monuments*, reformers like Latimer and
Ridley stand shoulder to shoulder with Mary Magdalene and St. Luke.
During the declining and degenerate periods of the church, these
witnesses kept alive and pure the faith misconstrued or prostituted by
an established church mired in error. In rehearsing the long and bloody
history of persecution in England, Foxe points out the general significance of the succession of martyrs in resolving one of the central
problems of Protestantism:

> And this was before the name of Luther was heard of in these countries
> among the people. Wherefore they are much beguiled and misinformed,
> who condemn this kind of doctrine now received, of novelty; asking, "Where
> was this church and religion forty years ago, before Luther's time?" To whom
> it may be answered, that this religion and form of doctrine was planted by the
> apostles, and taught by true bishops, afterward decayed, and now reformed
> again. Although it was not received nor admitted of the pope's clergy before
> Luther's time, neither yet is; yet it was received of others, in whose heart it
> pleased the Lord secretly to work; and that of a great number, who both
> professed and suffered for the same, as in the former times of this history may
> appear. (4:217)

While the Roman Catholic church was led astray by papal dreams of
worldly wealth and dominion, the true church of Christ survived with
the martyrs as its witness, and nowhere did it survive so successfully as
in England.

The Question of Nationalism

The question of the nature of Foxe's nationalism in the *Acts and
Monuments* has been much debated, especially since William Haller
theorized that Foxe's book was designed to convince the English that

their nation was the new Israel, God's "elect nation," destined to play a crucial part in the final, decisive struggle and overthrow of Antichrist.[29] However significant one considers the religio-nationalistic dimension of the book, Foxe is clear in his emphasis on England's importance in the history of the true church. First, he traces the pedigree of the English church back from the reformers of his day, past Luther to the Lollards, to Bede and his record of English saints, back to Roman Britain, where Christ's church was established in pristine purity, a genealogy recapitulated in brief in the preface "To the True and Faithful Congregation of Christ's Universal Church" which was added in 1570 when Foxe extended his history back to the time of Christ. He comes to discuss "domestical histories" at the beginning of book 2 where he explains the establishment of Christianity in Britain. Here he adduces the testimony of Gildas for a direct apostolic connection through the missionary work of Joseph of Arimathea in Britain and suggests that the faith came to Britain from the Greeks of the Eastern church rather than through the less pure Roman tradition. By the second century A.D., England already had its first Christian monarch, King Lucius, who sent to Eleutherius, bishop of Rome, for evangelists to help spread the faith already established in Britain. From thence Foxe traces the succession down a familiar path, through the British-born Constantine to Augustine and the Saxons, who, Foxe proves to his own satisfaction through an examination of a sermon by Aelfric, kept the authentic faith despite the corruption of the Roman church, through the resistance of England's medieval monarchs, especially Henry II, King John, and Edward I, to the rekindling of the light by Wycliffe and his followers. The English church then follows an ecclesiastical tradition at least as old and a good deal more pure than the Roman Catholic one, according to Foxe's history; and at the period when it did borrow from the Roman order, in the early times of Eleutherius and Augustine, the Roman church was still relatively uncorrupted. And throughout the declining age of the church, English monarchs resisted Roman pressure, English ecclesiastics fought against the innovations of Rome, and a steady stream of martyrs died for the pure faith harbored in England. In sum, Foxe argues throughout that the English church is ancient and true, the Roman novel and corrupt.

In the dark period before Henry VIII finally barred papal authority in England, the flower of the English church was the host of English martyrs who gave their lives as witness to the faith, for as Foxe affirms, "there hath been no region or country more fertile or fruitful for martyrs, than our own region of England. Whether it happeneth or cometh by the singular gift or privilege of God's divine grace, or else through the barbarous and foolish cruelty of such as at that time ruled and governed the church, it is uncertain" (3:581). The knowledge of these glorious anti-Roman martyrs and of the history of the true English church has long been obscured and distorted by monkish chroniclers and foreign historians. Foxe writes to restore this birthright to the English people, and indeed, as he explains to the queen in his dedication to her, he elects to write in the popular tongue out of "the necessity of the ignorant flock of Christ committed to your government in this realm of England; who, as they have been long led in ignorance, and wrapped in blindness, for lack especially of God's word, and partly also for wanting the light of history, I thought pity but that such should be helped, their ignorance relieved, and simplicity instructed" (1:viii). The English church is not only the most ancient and pure, but also the most glorious by virtue of the native martyrs whose blood has fed it; under Elizabeth, the reformed, or rather restored, English church should be a model for all nations. For in Foxe's account, Elizabeth follows her father's lead as the latest and most successful of "the imperial tradition" of monarchs who have resisted papal encroachment upon their sovereignties down through history.

The Central Message of Protestantism and the Primacy of the Word

The *Acts and Monuments* is then a book deeply imbued with patriotic feeling that has as at least a partial aim the instilling of nationalistic pride in its English audience. The larger purpose of the book, however, is to set forth the true history of Christ's universal church according to the reformer's view, tracing the essential elements of the apostolic church through the early church into the byways and outposts where it survived during what Foxe regards as the visible, established church's papal captivity, and back into the open with the reformed creed preached by Wycliffe, Hus, Jerome of Prague, and others, along with an account of the martyrs who testified to the true faith. Obviously, this history must be a universal one. England may be a principal actor, but often in the course of history both her rulers and her established church have departed from the truth. Even in Foxe's own day, warmed by the bright promise of Elizabeth's Protestant reign, as T. H. L. Parker observes, there is no evidence that Foxe is ever in danger of confusing the Kingdom of God with the realm ruled by Queen Elizabeth.[30] If the *Actes and Monuments* is regarded as an inspired piece of propaganda and and Foxe as "the first great journalist in English history," as Hugh Massingham calls him,[31] the cause he proselytizes for and the central message his great book preaches is not nationalism but Protestantism.

The fundamental principles of the reformed religion reticulate and reverberate through the pages of Foxe's book with such regular insistence that not even an indifferent reader could come away from browsing through it without an exposure to a primer on Protestantism. For in Foxe's view, sixteenth-century Protestantism may be regarded as a mirror of biblical Christianity. Thus it follows that "if martyrs are to be compared with martyrs, I see no cause why the martyrs of our time deserve any less commendation than the others in the primitive church," Foxe argues, because they witness to the same truths, the same doctrine enshrined in the Scriptures (1:xxviii). Here is the greatest of the fundamental Protestant principles enunciated throughout the *Acts and Monuments:* the primacy of the Word, the record of the pure and original church established by Christ contained in the Bible. As Geraldine V. Thompson suggests, "At the most profound level the Word is, for Foxe and his martyrs, tantamount to the primary sacrament."[32] The Protestants insist on free access to the Scriptures and the right to interpret them without clerical mediation, utilizing the words of the Scripture as infallible guides each individual should read and act upon. So, in a speech that can be repeatedly paralleled in the *Acts and Monuments,* the Marian martyr John Philpot, not an uneducated man, will not discourse of ecclesiastical traditions, commentators, and the like, excusing himself to his examiner: "whereas you would have me follow better learned men than myself: indeed I acknowledge that you, with a great many others, are far better learned than I, whose books, in respect of learning, I am not worthy to carry after you. But faith and the wisdom of God consist not in learning only, and therefore St. Paul willeth that our faith be not grounded upon the wisdom of man. If you can show by learning out of God's book, that I ought to be of another faith than I am, I will hear you and any other man whatsoever he be" (7:660).

Although the level of discourse may change, as in Foxe's account of the execution of one of the Marian martyrs named Mandrel, the insistence on the literal words of "God's book" does not:

> Mandrel, standing at the stake . . . Dr. Jeffrey the chancellor spoke to him, wishing him to yield to the doctors, who many hundred years had taught otherwise than he doth believe, etc. To whom Mandrel answered, "Master chancellor," said he, "trouble me with none of your doctors, whatsoever they say; but bring me the book of God, the Old Testament and the New, and I will answer you." "What sayest thou, Mandrel," quod he, "by the saints in the church, the image of our Lady, of the crucifix, and other holy saints? be they necessary?" etc. "Yes, master chancellor," said he, "very necessary to roast a shoulder of mutton." (8:725)

Given this unshakeable reliance solely on the Scriptures, the martyrs' examinations often appear ritualistic and repetitive, punctuated occasionally by a frustrated outburst such as that by Dr. Story, one of the principal Marian inquisitors, to a steadfast gospeller: "Bible-babble, bible-babble! What speakest thou of the bible?" (8:340).

Typically, the examinations of the Tudor martyrs proceeded through such cross-talk until the key doctrinal questions of the nature of the Eucharist and of the authority of the papacy were put directly to the witness, who upon denying the mass or the validity of the papacy was condemned for heresy. According to Bishop Nicholas Ridley these two, the corrupt mass and the usurped papacy, are the "main pillars holding up the synagogue of Satan" (7:425). The Protestants argued that neither the institution and primacy of the pope nor the doctrine of transubstantiation and the Roman manner of celebrating the mass, under only one kind with the host elevated for adoration, had any scriptural warrant. For Foxe and most reformers, the Eucharist was a commemorative, symbolic service and the head of the church was Christ in Heaven and monarchs and national bishops on earth. Foxe turns back to David and Solomon in the Old Testament for patterns of the strong godly monarch who appointed priests and reformed religion when necessary. In Christian times, the Emperor Constantine was a model of such monarchs, and Foxe's comparison of Elizabeth to the emperor in his dedication of 1563 clearly expresses his hopes for her rule. On the other hand, Peter was not preeminent among the apostles, and Christ gave him no special charter, certainly not one that might be successively inherited, as head of his church on earth; papal pretensions were a sham. As for the celebration of the Eucharist, Foxe structures an historical argument to press his claim that the original ceremony has been blurred and festooned with merely human accretions in the Roman Catholic ritual, including most notoriously the doctrine of transubstantiation which Foxe attempts to dismiss as a late medieval innovation unknown in the original church. Most deplorable of all to Foxe, the Eucharist, a celebration of love and communion between men and God, has been turned by the papists into a savage litmus test of orthodoxy, a key weapon against reformers.[33] Justification by faith alone, the importance of a preaching clergy, and other familiar Protestant positions are traced historically, explained, defended, and repeated so often in the *Acts and Monuments* as to validate Helen C. White's characterization of the work as "an encyclopedia of the Reformation in England."[34]

Thus in the nearly twenty years from the inception of the Lollard martyrology through the completion of the two-volume 1570 *Ecclesiastical History,* Foxe tested, expanded, and shaped the design of the *Acts and Monuments* to provide Englishmen with a distinctive way of viewing the Protestant church and the martyrs who were its greatest glory. Further, Foxe's work became, in Frances Yates's description, "the prism through which many Elizabethans saw the history of their country."[35] Drawing on his wide reading and tireless study, Foxe developed and defended his conception of the martyrs and the church of the elect for which they died. Within the overarching periodization of history he worked out in the *Acts and Monuments,* Foxe paid special attention to the role of England in the history of the church in nurturing and harboring the true faith in hostile times and offering up a shining procession of witnesses through the ages to seal the truth with their blood. In brief, Foxe worked out a defense of Protestantism, "the classic statement of the ideology of the English Reformation" one recent critic calls it,[36] complete with a Protestant martyrology and ecclesiology in opposition to the Roman Catholic ones in a work with a strong nationalistic tinge; such a feat accounts for the initial popularity of the work in an age eager for just the answers Foxe offered. But for the enduring pleasure that made the work continually popular for centuries with English readers, it is necessary to consider the literary artistry with which Foxe filled in the particulars on the vast canvas of his ecclesiastical history, the skills that brought the individual martyrs and monarchs alive to fire the blood of generations of English readers.

Chapter Three
The *Acts and Monuments:* Literature and Propaganda

The Protestant Encyclopedia

The breadth and range of appeal of the *Acts and Monuments* in Renaissance England cannot be overestimated. From the ordinary citizen who knew it as one of the four chained books in the cathedrals and many parish churches to the great and the near-great, like Sir Francis Drake who took a copy on his circumnavigation in 1577, the *Acts and Monuments* met an enthusiastic reception in Protestant England. In assessing the eight volumes of the stolid Victorian edition reprinted for the twentieth century in dull maroon library bindings, the modern reader needs to recall the original massive black folios, printed with packed columns of black-letter text. To the Elizabethans, they were almost as authoritative and often as moving as the Bible itself. The minute attention these old folios received is witnessed by margins crammed with the scribbled comments of past generations of readers, favorite passages underlined, and pictures worn with handling. These are the hallmarks of a book not read as a public or religious duty but as a revered work which inspired personal devotion and strengthened faith, a terrible and glorious record.

As such a record, the work succeeded even better than Foxe had hoped. He saw himself as an historian, tracing the true church through the thickets and brambles of a hostile world. Yet his grand dialectical pattern, tracing the struggle between God and Satan as waged by their agents in this world over a 1,500-year period, was so loose as to admit of all sorts of varied material. Thus the history Foxe actually wrote is also a Protestant martyrology, with closer ties to the Catholic tradition of hagiography than its author would admit,[1] an encyclopedia of Protestantism with an index providing immediate access to all the primary issues of the Reformation, an Erastian political tract, an enormous diatribe ("the longest pamphlet ever composed by the hand of man," one hostile critic calls it)[2] against Roman Catholicism, and, in fact, an anatomy of persecution. As an anatomy, Foxe's book includes a medley of literary forms, in prose and verse, ranging from sermons, tracts, and epistles to doggerel rimes, self-contained stories of romantic adventure, such as the story of the duchess of Suffolk racing in disguise around the Continent, and comic ones, like the imagined fire at Cambridge in 1541 which illustrates how foolish supposedly wise men might be. Beast fables, mock-epistles, moments of high dramatic conflict, and scenes of heart-wrenching pathos, all find space in Foxe's narrative; it must have been a rare Protestant reader who could find nothing to suit him in the *Acts and Monuments*.

To Elizabethan readers, much of Foxe's material was as fresh and timely as our news magazines, which helps to explain why the portions of this gallimaufry of subjects and literary forms favored by Renaissance readers often differ from the modern appreciation of the *Acts and Monuments*. In particular, the great mass of Henrician and Marian materials on theological disputation Foxe includes is essentially unattractive to modern audiences due to its tedious repetition, nondramatic nature, and technical language. But to a Renaissance audience, trained from grammar school in the arts of grammar, rhetoric, and logic, the well-knit argument forcefully urged was a high form of entertainment as well as instruction. And judging from the kinds of works printed by English publishers during the Renaissance, the preponderance of religious titles featuring theological disputations, sermons, tracts, glosses, and commentaries, Reformation controversy, Foxe's chief subject matter, could hardly have been more popular. Evidence is abundant that Foxe's original audience followed these lengthy debates and tracts closely. For instance, Foxe notes in passing that when the bishop of Winchester was examined formally on the grounds of his faith in the reign of Edward VI, some twenty or so auditors of a sermon he had delivered at Paul's Cross were brought in to testify as to what points Winchester had made. The testimony of these men—carpenters, tanners, and tradesmen, not theologians or scholars—reveals that most took notes and even outlined the sermon as it was being delivered. And, of course, the thrust and parry of theological dispute was heightened for early readers not only by their knowledge of the stakes involved, often a slow, horrible death for the vanquished, but by the fear that with another change in governments and religion, they themselves might be required to stand to similar tests.

Nevertheless, while Foxe's early readers often appreciated his book in a fashion different from moderns, the center of interest for most readers from Foxe's day to ours ultimately is the same: a focus on the final acts, the last witness of the Christian martyrs at the time of their execution. The most memorable scenes are those at the stake, where occur the unforgettable speeches such as Tyndale's dying plea, "Lord! open the king of England's eyes," or Latimer's encouragement to "Be of good comfort, master Ridley, and play the man. We shall this day light such a candle, by God's grace, in England, as I trust shall never be put out." The engravers commissioned to provide woodcuts for the text recognized this elemental appeal and made not the apprehension, examination, or torture of the martyrs their chief subject but the moment of death, the collision of fire, flesh, and spirit. And Foxe's genius for description is nowhere more evident than in the clinical description and emotional interpretation of the final scenes at the stake; he is, as H. C. White observes, "a master of horror."[3]

Foxe's concentration on the final witness of the martyrs and their preparations for the ordeal suggests another reason for the popularity of the *Acts and Monuments*; it teaches a valuable, practical lesson every reader can apply to his own life: the art of dying well in the Christian faith. Thus, generically the *Acts and Monuments* may be considered not only as a history, martyrology, Protestant encyclopedia, and anatomy of persecution, but also as a Renaissance courtesy book teaching proper conduct. It differs from such popular examples of Renaissance conduct manuals as Castiglione's *Book of the Courtier* or Peacham's *Compleat Gentleman* in its focus not only on how to live well according to an approved code of behavior but how to die well so as to authenticate the faith that has guided an individual's life. As a richly detailed Protestant contribution to the still flourishing *ars moriendi* literature of the Catholic Middle Ages, Foxe's *Acts and Monuments* supplements and, in fact, completes the Reformers' guides for holy living and worship with his stories of heroic Protestant martyrs.[4]

The Art of Holy Dying

During the sixteenth century the manner of a person's conduct at his death was widely regarded as final evidence of the worth or validity of the rule by which he lived his life, and consequently the different religious factions were united especially in their scrutiny of the death scenes of those executed for their faith. Thus a sizeable crowd could be counted on at public executions for religion's sake, the spectators divided along sectarian lines and often as vociferous in their sentiments as crowds at sporting contests. Foxe frequently includes descriptions of audience reaction, as at the burning of Kerby at Ipswich before "a great number of people, about two thousand by estimation," where he died so well, steadfastly praying to God in the flames, that the persecutors themselves wept, all the while "the people giving shouts, and praising God with great admiration of his constancy, being so simple and unlettered" (5:531–32). Foxe supplements his textual description and approval of such heroic Christian deaths with marginal glosses like "Note the quick and joyful death of this blessed martyr" (5:573), and he is quick to point the difference between the final actions of true martyrs and common criminals marked for execution: "For whereas they who suffer as malefactors, are commonly wont to go heavy and pensive to their death, so the others, with heavenly alacrity and cheerfulness, do abide whatsoever it pleaseth the Lord to lay upon them" (5:438).

All concerned in the religious persecutions, then, were aware of the importance of the victim's conduct at his execution; the good death constituted, as Foxe asserts, "a plain, visible argument" (7:667) for the truth of the victim's sustaining faith. Thus the temptations of the martyrs extended through to the final scene, when even after the flames were lit the martyr could yet buy his life, sometimes even his freedom, by kissing a proffered crucifix or recanting his reformed faith. Fully aware of their mortal frailty, martyrs prayed for strength of will to subdue the rebellious flesh. Some even prepared for the stake physically as well as spiritually by testing their final opponent, devouring fire. Some tested themselves by holding their hands over a candle; Thomas Bilney burned off an entire digit of one finger in such an exercise, pitting his will against his flesh. Another, George Tankerfield, burned in 1555, graphically illustrates the martyrs' fear that their flesh will betray their faith. Foxe records how the night before Tankerfield's execution

> he prayed his host to let him have a good fire in the chamber; he had so, and then he, sitting on a form before the fire, put off his shoes and hose, and stretched out his leg to the flame; and when it had touched his foot, he quickly withdrew his leg, showing how the flesh did persuade him one way, and the spirit another way. The flesh said, "O thou fool, wilt thou burn and heedest not?" The spirit said, "Be not afraid, for this is nothing, in respect of fire eternal." The flesh said, "Do not leave the company of thy friends and acquaintance which love thee, and will let thee lack nothing." The spirit said, "The company of Jesus Christ and his glorious presence doth exceed all fleshly friends." The flesh said, "Do not shorten thy time, for thou mayest live, if thou wilt, much longer." The spirit said, "This life is nothing unto the life in heaven, which lasteth forever," etc. (7:346)

As proof of victory over the flesh and confirmation of the good death, the martyrs were often asked for a sign or token of their victory in the flames. For example, prior to the execution of the Welsh reformer Robert Ferrar, bishop of St. David's, "one named Richard Jones, a knight's son, coming to master Ferrar a little before his death, seemed to lament the painfulness of the death he had to suffer: unto whom the bishop answered again to the effect, saying, that if he saw him once to stir in the pains of his burning, he should then give no credit to his doctrine. And as he said; for so patiently he stood, that he never moved, but even as he stood (holding up his stumps), so still he continued, till one Richard Gravell with a staff dashed him upon the head, and so struck him down" (7:26). These significations were considered extremely efficacious in bolstering the faith and fortifying the determination of bystanders; examples of final tokens are so common in Foxe's account as to suggest that as ritualistic actions they were meant to provide a palpable substitute for the fantastic miracles of the old saints in the discredited tradition of *The Golden Legend*. When Foxe writes over and over of how some miserable soul, scarcely more than a lump of charcoal, rises from the inferno to signal the triumph of his faith to the onlookers, he certainly regards the action as a kind of ultimate proof, as in the case of Thomas Haukes, burned in 1555:

> A little before his death, certain there were of his familiar acquaintance and friends, who frequented his company more familiarly, who seemed not a

little to be confirmed both by the example of his constancy, and by his talk; yet notwithstanding, the same again, being feared with the sharpness of the punishment which he was going to, privily desired that in the midst of the flame he would show them some token, if he could, whereby they might be the more certain, whether the pain of such burning were so great that a man might not therein keep his mind quiet and patient. Which thing he promised them to do; and so, secretly between them, it was agreed that if the rage of the pain were tolerable and might be suffered, then he should lift up his hands over his head towards heaven, before he gave up the ghost . . . the fire was set to him. In the which when he continued long, and when his speech was taken away by violence of the flame, his skin also drawn together, and his fingers consumed with the fire, so that now all men thought certainly he had been gone, suddenly, and contrary to all expectation, the blessed servant of God, being mindful of his promise afore made, reached up his hands burning on a light fire, which was marvellous to behold, over his head to the living God, and with great rejoicing as it seemed, struck or clapped them three times together. . . . (7:3)

Indeed, even when no sign was promised, the bystanders, and Foxe's readers, examined the final actions of the victim closely. For example, Foxe records what witnesses watched for in the mutilation of William Flower, a former monk turned schoolteacher who had entered St. Margaret's Church in Westminster in 1555 and struck with a woodknife a priest preparing to offer up the sacrament. Prior to his burning, Foxe writes, "his right hand, being held up against the stake, was stricken off, his left hand being stayed behind him. At the which striking off his hand, certain that were present beholders of the matter, and purposely observing the same, credibly informed us, that he in no part of his body did once shrink at the striking thereof, but once a little he stirred his shoulders" (7:76).

The struggle between flesh and spirit is one every man can identify with, and Foxe expands repeatedly on the triumph of the will as a key element in the good Christian death. But having conquered the flesh and the natural fear of death, the martyr must satisfactorily resolve yet another internal conflict in order to win the crown of Christian martyrdom. Since death might often be avoided by various expedients, the persecuted Christian must examine the state of his mind and soul, the motives for his self-sacrifice, to determine whether death was the only correct and necessary option open to him. In brief, as in the *ars moriendi* literature, it is not only the external event, the actual burning, which is significant but the martyr's state of mind, his spiritual fortitude, fidelity, and willingness for self-sacrifice, which gives meaning to his final act. "The cause, not the pain, maketh a martyr" (6:6), Foxe writes, and the cause prompting a Christian to give himself to be burned as a witness becomes a major subject of interest in the *Acts and Monuments*.

Foxe's definition of a martyr as a "witness-bearer," willing to suffer to the end even though death might not be required, shifts attention to the psychology of martyrdom; the purity of the martyr's motives—the causes that lead him to risk all to testify to his faith—become in Foxe's narrative as important as the external event, the final conduct of those executed. In shifting emphasis from the gruesome details of the martyrs' end to the internal aspects of their voluntary witness, Foxe brought the *Acts and Monuments* into line with the *ars moriendi* tradition and fed the burgeoning Elizabethan interest in psychology and the relation between motive and act. In particular, the Tudor stories of martyrdom undergo an internalizing process as Foxe explores, often through their own words, not only the conflict between flesh and spirit but the divisions within the mind and soul of the Protestant martyrs. In the reports of examinations, letters, and eyewitness testimony which Foxe printed verbatim in his book, to authenticate it and dissociate it from the fabulous stories of the older Catholic saints, it is evident that even among the heroes many suffered periods of self-doubt and fears of insufficiency. In place of the one-dimensional saints of the old tradition, Foxe's Tudor martyrs reveal themselves to be believable representatives of flawed humanity striving for perfection in their faith. Some, like Archbishop Cranmer, finally broke under the pressure; others, such as John Bradford, endured periods of self-doubt described in letters to his friends signed by "A very painted hypocrite, John Bradford," "The sinful John Bradford," or simply "*miserrimus peccator*" (6:277, 284–85).

The martyrs agonized especially over the danger of suicide.[5] If they would succumb to the sort of religious melancholy to which the godly are most susceptible, they risk a despair which negates the purity of their witness to the faith. If, on the other hand, they run too rapidly to embrace a martyr's crown, ignoring other honest courses by which both life and faith might be preserved, self-pride or the egotistic desire for fame taints the sacrifice. Hence, intensive self-examination of motives and options is frequent among Foxe's martyrs. Thus for a number of the

Tudor martyrs, where the firsthand materials for such a study were available to Foxe, the area for his exploration, analysis, and dramatization is less the public disputation, the examination room, or the torture chamber, than the mind and heart of the individual Christian who must work his way through a lonely analysis to reach a conclusion upon which hangs the fate of his immortal soul.

In sum, much of the early popularity and practical utility of the *Acts and Monuments* derives from its function as a guide to godly conduct, especially as a vivid illustration of how to die well in the faith. Foxe drew upon and reworked the *ars moriendi* tradition within a Protestant context, emphasizing the spiritual and physical components of heroic Christian death. Through detailed description of the martyrs' executions, Foxe explores physical martyrdom as a witness and proof of faith. Here he varies from the *ars moriendi* tradition chiefly in the high degree of clinical, physiological detail he reports concerning the horrible manner of the martyrs' death. In moving from the physical to the psychological and spiritual, Foxe significantly internalizes the martyrs' struggles, embodying the precepts and guidelines of a Christian conduct book in strongly realized character studies of contemporary individuals. Just as the conduct of the martyrs at the stake provides a pattern for the average Christian to emulate, so the successful resolution of the internal conflict between flesh and spirit in the will of the individual and the deeper self-analysis of motive affords a paradigm no less fascinating than directly relevant to the inner life of all Christians. Foxe's martyrs are not plaster saints but flesh-and-blood humans, often wracked by doubts and fears. By reading accounts, often in the martyrs' own words, of how their faith in Christ conquered their fears of the fire without and the spiritual flaws within, the individual reader can fortify and prepare himself for the common end of all men. Foxe's martyrs are thus familiar, flesh-and-blood people whose triumph over fear, self-doubt, and despair to achieve notable godly deaths constitutes a lively demonstration and potent argument for the Reformed faith.

The Reinforcement by Visual Icon

While the function of the *Acts and Monuments* as a Protestant guide to godly dying explains one important element in the popularity of the work, another major feature of its appeal is the technical presentation of

Foxe's narrative. In addition to the massive and authoritarian appearance of the oversize, double-columned folios, Foxe's record was physically imposing and appealing as a visual artifact. From the engraved title page, iconographically representing the theme of the work with the martyrs ascending to their heavenly reward on one side and the persecuting papists tumbling down to the waiting devils of Hell along the other, to the more than 160 illustrations in the editions of the 1570s and later, the pictures constituted a potent nonverbal argument accessible even to the illiterate. As such, they were an essential complement to the textual descriptions of the martyrs' deaths Foxe had claimed were "a plain, visible argument" more moving than volumes of polemic. Foxe often coordinated his text with the engravings he had commissioned, calling the reader's attention to specific illustrations, the verbal and visual clarifying and reinforcing each other.[6]

The engravings in the *Acts and Monuments* fall into three fairly clearly distinguishable groups, as George Williamson notes in his edition.[7] First, there are the small conventional engravings of martyrs which are scattered throughout the text. The same engravings are used repeatedly for different martyrs without any pretense of being original portraits of individual martyrs (although the names are changed for each). These engravings of martyrs peering heavenward through the flames thus help to universalize the individual martyrs by graphically reminding the reader how the sacrifice of these countrymen has identified them with all those who have ever died for Christ. The second group is composed of larger, more formal engravings combining realistic with allegorical techniques, such as the engraving of Henry VIII trampling the pope.[8] Finally, the most interesting group is composed of realistic engravings of people and events evidently designed from eyewitness reports. Examples of these realistic engravings include the scene of the burning of a group of Protestants at Windsor or the famous portrait of Bishop Bonner scourging a young Reformer in his garden while even his henchmen must cover their faces and look away out of pity. J. F. Mozley suggests that Foxe himself might have created the sketches on which some of these realistic engravings were based.[9] At any event, they are so accurate and moving that Bonner himself is said to have complained of the accuracy of the likeness.[10]

While the engravings are certainly the key feature and emotional center of the *Acts and Monuments* as a visual artifact, several other aspects of the early folios convey a strong visual impression. Francis Yates calls particular attention to the capital *C* which begins the dedication to the Elizabethan editions. It is an oversized engraved initial containing a picture of Queen Elizabeth enthroned. Above her, the top curve of the letter blossoms into a bountiful cornucopia; below her feet, the lower arc of the letter contains the pope, writhing in serpentine form. Thus, Yates argues, the illustrated initial "is the climax of the whole book,"[11] illustrating in miniature Elizabeth's assertion of the English imperial tradition over the pope. Another feature of the original 1563 edition which stirred a good deal of controversy was the Kalender of Martyrs and confessors featuring such Tudor Protestants as John Rogers and Laurence Saunders placed alongside St. Paul, Mary Magdalen, and St. Bartholomew. Greater and lesser martyrs were distinguished by printing their names in red and black ink respectively, an immediately striking feature as the only use of colored ink in the *Acts and Monuments*. Foxe seems to have been genuinely surprised at the attacks the Kalender provoked from those who accused him of either perpetuating or perverting the old Catholic saints' calendar under another guise. He dropped the Kalender from his editions of 1570 and 1576, but restored it in the 1583 edition. These various visual embellishments enriched the work for all readers, while for certain segments of Foxe's audience, the simple and unlettered, for example, or children, the primary impact of the great book chained in their churches was as a visual artifact whose engravings epitomized and drove home key themes and motifs.

Foxe's Art of Narrative

These themes, especially the central ones of martyrdom for the true faith and imperial resistance to papal pretension, are emphasized by Foxe's skillful management of his narrative. Occasionally, the twin themes come together, as in the case of Constantine, who Christianized the Roman Empire, reformed the church, and stayed persecution, or Thomas Cromwell, who worked equally hard for English independence from Rome and for the institutionalization of the Protestant faith. In such instances, Foxe gives relatively full biographies of the key figures, along with discussion of their significance. When the two themes do not coalesce neatly about a key figure, Foxe often alternates tracing one, then the other, with copious historical illustrations of brave people, from parish priests, sheriffs, and private citizens through ministers of state and monarchs like King John or Edward III. The kings defied Roman claims and refused Roman extortion while the people risked and often forfeited their lives to keep the true apostolic faith alive in times of apostacy. These humble people, many of them faceless and even nameless in Foxe's narration, provide a continuity that keeps the central themes before the reader's eye even through pages of documents, reports, and other data.

Arising from the background stories of these people who attract Foxe's attention for a brief period due to some act, speech, or opinion they hold are the large, "tent-post" figures who enter the narrative at crucial points. These figures receive extended biographical treatment, often covering the entire life, as well as a discussion of their significance in the course of history. They thus constitute a link between Foxe's history and the older chronicle histories organized around sketches of rulers and great men treated as positive and negative moral exampla. When he arrives at the history of the Tudor period, about midway through the *Acts and Monuments,* where records are plentiful and the theology is unambiguously Protestant, Foxe slows his pace and he offers more of these full-scale biographies of such central figures as Cromwell, Latimer, Tyndale, and Cranmer on the one side and Wolsey, Winchester, and Bonner on the other. Since for Foxe these men are obviously agents in the universal struggle between God and Satan, he naturally appends a moral interpretation of the quality of their lives, and deaths, to the narrative of their deeds.

Foxe's historical canvas is designed to conduct the reader from the fragmentary to the complete, from partial to whole understanding. The journey begins with the unedifying background and atmosphere of fallen humanity, where the struggles even between popes and monarchs often seem merely venal. Out of this flux of human history arises a group of people who emerge from obscurity to strike blows for the neglected true faith and against papal claims of dominion. The meaning of the fragmentary stories of these people, martyrs and witnesses whom Foxe chronicles as a true thread through the tangle of history, becomes clear in the full-scale treatment accorded the major figures in the narrative. By the very historical prominence of these "tent-post" figures, they are recognized by Foxe as deliberate agents of greater powers, tools in the struggle between God and Satan waged on earth.[12] Thus, the positions taken by relatively anonymous individuals emerge from the confused background of historical struggle as beacons whose true light receives confirmation and added luster from the presentation of the great figures who occupy the world's stage. The two groups of private and public witnesses both echo and reinforce each other. Finally, when the characters of both background and foreground are viewed from the larger, metaphysical perspective which alone makes their stands comprehensible, human action is shown by Foxe to be a visible, earthly manifestation of the ongoing struggle between Good and Evil in the universe. From this complete perspective with each layer of action illumining its fellow, the reader can place the individual martyr into a proper context, elevating the quotidian to the eternal, as such differentia as age, sex, and geography melt away and as all are divided into one of two camps, shoulder to shoulder with their comrades of other eras and climes.

As the stories of lesser figures feed into those of greater in the web of Foxe's narrative, so the principle of echoing parallel and analogy becomes an important unifying device in the work. A handful of central themes and motifs are embodied in story after story until the reader is assured of being on relatively familiar ground wherever he opens the volume. The repetition of the acts of defiance and sacrifice through the ages ultimately suggests their timeless, ritualistic aspect and encourages the substitution of an apocalyptic perspective for the secular temporal one of human history. Both the martyrs and their persecutors are distinguished by the essential spiritual traits they share regardless of era or country. Thus, for example, Hugh Latimer has far more in common with the Roman Polycarp martyred 1,500 years earlier than he does with his sometime fellow Tudor bishop Stephen Gardiner, as Latimer seeks to suggest by paraphrasing at the stake the famous injunction heard at Polycarp's execution. The reader need not remember all the details and names of the witnesses, for they become types, as Foxe continually suggests by comparing martyrs with those of other times, as Tudor with Roman or with biblical figures, until the martyrs' stories seem almost an extension of the Scriptures themselves.[13] What appears at first reading to be an incredible medley of stories, pictures, styles, and literary types soon comes into focus as a structured polyphony whose inner harmony emerges from the dissonance. Thus the key themes are brought home more by repetition than any sense of strong forward movement, even within Foxe's cyclic and apocalpytic chronological frame.

Inevitably the realistic detail and palpable surface descriptions of individual martyrs and witnesses continually yield to actions and attitudes more typical than idiosyncratic, as Foxe compares individuals on a spiritual basis rather than an historical or geographical one. Thus, the fortitude of Laurence Saunders in the flames of Smithfield suggests to Foxe the courage of St. Laurence at his roasting or the horrible ordeal of Bishop Hooper in the fire recalls Polycarp's martyrdom, prompting Foxe to an extended comparison of ancient and modern martyrs. More extensive still is Foxe's typological reading of the Old Testament, in whose history of the Israelites "we shall see a lively representation of these our days expressed in that prophetical people, according as St. Paul, writing of them showeth how all things happened to them in figures, that is, the actions and doings of that one nation, be as figures and types of greater matters, what shall happen in the latter times of the whole church universally in Christ collected" (4:95). Thus, it is only natural for Foxe to compare persecution of English Lollards by both church and state to the Israelites suffering under Pharaoh or modern figures to biblical ones, as Edward VI is compared throughout the *Acts and Monuments* to the young Israelite monarch Josias.[14] Indeed, so reflexive does this analogical habit become on Foxe's part that he occasionally overdoes it. In the 1563 edition, for example, Foxe designed the story of the fall and end of Protector Somerset so distinctly as an *imitatio Christi* that in the edition of 1570 he was constrained to include a note of disclaimer in his preface: "Itē, here also is to be noted touchyng ye sayd Duke of Somerset, that albeit at hys death relation is made of a sodeine fallyng of the people, as was at the takyng of Christ, this is not to be expounded as though I compared in any part the Duke of Somerset with Christ."[15] This habitual recourse to analogy in describing the actions of people in the *Acts and Monuments* is another way in which Foxe gathers up the local and temporal into the stream of dialectical history.

The great strength of Foxe's presentation of both the martyrs and their adversaries, then, is his ability to describe each individual as both unique and simultaneously representative of a large class, as a symbol but not an abstraction. Indeed, the "vivid reality"[16] of Foxe's descriptions is so often praised that a brief examination may be useful to illustrate how biographical strategy is managed in the presentation of major and minor figures in the work. In the handling of major, "tent-post" figures, Foxe's characterization reflects the polarity of his world view; major figures are seldom presented as admixtures of good and bad traits. Instead, despite the wealth of documentary source material, often including idiosyncratic personal detail, it is their exemplary value Foxe prizes.[17] Beneath the realistic surface of his story, saints and demons are locked in mortal conflict. Thus, in describing his major heroes, the attraction of the hagiographic paradigm is enormously strong even when Foxe seeks to resist it as in his account of the career of Martin Luther. "Those who write the lives of saints use to describe and extol their holy life and godly virtues, and also to set forth such miracles as be wrought in them by God; whereof there lacketh no plenty in Martin Luther, but rather time lacketh to us, and opportunity to tarry upon them, having such haste to other things. Otherwise what a miracle might this seem to be, for one man, and a poor friar, creeping out of a blind cloister, to be set up against the pope," Foxe writes (4:318–19), as he proceeds to describe various particularly miraculous preservations of Luther from his enemies. Similarly, the temptation to present the adversaries of the true church not just as misguided or even evil men, but as demi-demons, is clearly seen in such passages as Foxe's description of Winchester's putative deformity, another illustration of Foxe's use of paralipsis, the rhetorical figure in which the speaker effectively tells what he pretends to pass over: "I will not here speak of that which hath been constantly reported to me touching the monstrous making and mishapen fashion of his feet and toes, the nails whereof were said not to be like to other men's, but to crook downward, and to be sharp like the claws of ravening beasts" (7:586).

The realistic surface detail of Foxe's stories is tactical; the shaping spirit of the history around frankly partisan exemplary figures is strategic. Foxe's respect for factual evidence functions as a check upon the tendency to moralize history (note that the interpretation of fact, as in Luther's "miraculous" escapes, and hearsay, as in Winchester's extremities, are both pretty clearly labeled for what they are). In the biographies of "tent-post" characters through the arrangement of detail and authorial interpretation and commentary, Foxe slants major figures to serve the ends of his dialectic. Pope Gregory VII, Hildebrand, who was instrumental in banning clerical marriage and advancing Roman Catholic power into the temporal realm, is an example of Foxe's hostile biographical strategy. He relates the "acts and facts" of Hildebrand's career complete with supporting documents, all interpreted in negative fashion, even down to his name which Foxe suggests should have been Hellbrand. Finally, Foxe summarizes Hildebrand's historical importance and role in the cosmic conflict between Good and Evil and the two churches which represent them on earth.

Of course, the initial decision to include a full biographical sketch of a figure may be the result of its exemplary potential. After his lengthy consideration of Hildebrand, for example, Foxe considers the English monarchs of the period; but here some, such as King William Rufus, receive comparatively scant attention for, Foxe observes, "Hys lyfe was such, that it is hard for a story: that should tell truth, to say, whether he was more to be commended, or reproved."[18] On the other hand, Cardinal Wolsey receives featured biographical treatment precisely because he is such a splendid exemplary figure. Foxe apologizes for the inclusion of this biography, "although it be not greatly pertinent unto this our history," as the definitive portrait of a proud prelate: "For like as the Lacademonians, in times past, were accustomed to show and demonstrate drunken men unto their children, to behold and look upon, that through the foulness of that vice, they might inflame them the more to the study and desire of sobriety; even so it shall not be hurtful sometimes to set forth the examples which are not honest, that others might thereby gather the instruction of better and more upright dealing" (4:588).

Thus because of their importance in the conflict between God and Satan, the "tent-post" characters typically receive a full biographical treatment which springs from a faithful adherence to historical fact and particular detail. Yet the requirement of Foxe's commitment to Protestant history demands that the facts be interpreted and presented so that the moral dimension of his characters' lives is immediately apparent. The strain on the narrative of this double commitment is often evident. Thomas Cromwell, for example, is one of Foxe's great Tudor heroes. His story is related with scrupulous concern for documentary fact and a sharp eye for authentic detail, as in the vivid, anecdotal quality of Foxe's account of a near-tragedy at a bear-baiting held on the Thames. At the same time, however, Foxe assiduously builds Cromwell up as a kind of Protestant Thomas More, a gifted politician, thinker, peacemaker, one who is widely admired and beloved. Foxe lists Cromwell's heroic qualities and stresses his divine warrant in suppressing the religious houses when "Almighty God (who cannot forget his promise) provided remedy in time, in raising up this Cromwell his servant, and other like champions" (5:376). Foxe even accords him an heroic sobriquet; he is the *"malleus monachorum,"* the hammer of monks. In this and similar instances, Foxe is clearly endeavoring to transform historical figures into mythic types, the champions he speaks of supported by "God's special providence and secret guiding" (5:378).

The process of mythic transformation in key biographical sketches is, if anything, even more evident in Foxe's treatment of his central villains. The modern Protestant's enemies, he asserts, are those foretold by the apostles, the three capital adversaries "signified in the Apocalypse by the beast, the false lamb, and the false prophet," whom Foxe reveals as the heathen emperors, the barbarous Turk, and the proud pope (4:79). And if Cromwell and God's other champions receive divine aid, it is no less certain that Satan's minions, like Winchester of the bestial extremities, receive his full support and bear his mark. Indeed, Foxe is as aware as any storyteller or dramatist of his age of the importance of a larger-than-life villain to be both feared and hissed by his audience. Thus, it should come as no surprise that of all the hundreds of characters in the *Acts and Monuments,* the one who receives the most attention, the most space, is not one of Foxe's martyrs or heroic monarchs but a villain, Stephen Gardiner, bishop of Winchester. Foxe bestows upon "wily Winchester" an iniquitous epithet that defines his character as duplicitous, false, and cunning, even while the narrative associates him with Wolsey, that symbol of "proud prelacy," and the reader comes to see Winchester in his evasions and misconstructions as a native English representation of the Roman popes, identified earlier by Foxe as Antichrist. Elevated to Lord Chancellor upon the succession of Mary, Winchester works in tandem with Edmund Bonner, Foxe's "bloody Bonner," bishop of London, as the domestic representative of Antichrist's other outstanding trait, his bestial cruelty. For Foxe,

Bonner is so blood-thirsty that he cannot be surfeited; unlike the more cerebral Winchester, Bonner takes a direct role in the tortures and executions of Protestants. Foxe's accounts of Bonner's persecution are often so vividly overwritten that Bonner frequently ceases to be human at all. In recounting Bonner's method of personally scourging unfortunate Protestants, including children, in his garden, Foxe tells the story of one youth whom Bonner could not drive to recant his faith through whipping, asserting that "Oftimes speaking of the said John Milles, he would say, 'They call me bloody Bonner. A vengeance on you all! I would fain be rid of you, but you have a delight in burning. But if I might have my will, I would sew your mouths, and put you in sacks and drown you!'" (8:486). In such passages, Foxe transforms Bonner from an historical figure into a cartoon villain, and modern historians complain with some justice of the distorted presentation.[19] Another way in which Foxe turns the bishop of London into a dehumanized, devouring monster is through the use of bestial imagery to describe him, a technique he may have borrowed from the martyrs themselves, as in John Bradford's letter from prison caricaturing Bonner:

My Lord, I thought it good to tarry a time until your lordship's stomach were come to you a little better; for I do perceive by your great fat cheeks, that you lack no lamb's flesh yet, and belike you are almost glutted with supping so much blood, and therefore you will let some of the leanest die in prison, which will then be meat good enough for your barking beagles, Harpsfield and his fellows. But yet, my lord, it were a great deal more for your lordship's honour, if your chaplains might have the meat roasted in Smithfield at the fire of the stake, yea, and when it is something fat and fair-liking; for now they have nothing but skin and bones, and if the dogs come hastily to it, they may chance shortly to be choaked; and then your hunting will be hindered greatly, if it be not altogether marred. (7:8)

Foxe then is certainly guilty of slanting, sometimes to the verge of caricature, his major characters. Yet, on Foxe's behalf, it should be noted that the slanting, the tendency to base characterization upon moral stereotypes, is less an attempt to deceive than to stir the reader; Foxe presents himself quite frankly as an involved, passionate, and partisan historian. His beliefs and sympathies are stated openly and the sources of his information are noted even when, as in the case of

Winchester's supposed bestial feet, they are only hearsay. It is thus possible to defend even Foxe's slanted characterizations on the grounds, as George Williamson argues, that

His beliefs were so genuine and so strong that they could not be left out of the picture in the name of impartiality! Partisan writing is far less dangerous; it need not be misleading, and partiality does not destroy objectivity. . . . If we read a writer whose bias is evident, we shall not be deceived; if we read one whose impartiality is only bias disguised, we shall be led far astray. It may unhesitatingly be asserted that Foxe was an entirely honest man who made every effort to collect reliable information from all possible sources, and to record facts.[20]

If this apologia seems overingenuous, it is nevertheless true that in the presentation of his major characters Foxe creates a dynamic tension between impartial historical fact upon which the biographical sketches are constructed and the overlay of interpretive commentary and hearsay evidence, included even when labeled as of dubious validity. The artistic advantages of this scheme of characterization are readily obvious. Foxe heightens and polarizes the dialectical clash of men and ideas, the biographical sketches reinforcing what H. C. White calls the "crusade psychology" of the *Acts and Monuments*.[21] The factual base suggests to the Protestant reader that he is receiving an accurate record of historical fact rather than an amalgam of legendary materials such as filled the medieval Catholic saints' lives. And the authoritative narrative voice, like a dependable friend at his elbow, guiding and interpreting for the reader the proper perspective on the events in history, works on the emotions, evoking pity, outrage, horror, or whatever response a story calls for.

In addition to the importance of the slanted characterization in making the narrative more vivid and dramatic, the tendency to nudge historical figures into moral and social stereotypes could even, in Foxe's hands, transform the public perception of living individuals and so entice them to conform to the historian's portrait. After six years as monarch, Queen Elizabeth was still relatively new to the throne when Foxe's biographical sketch of her appeared in the *Acts and Monuments*. The historian was apprehensive about including a narrative of her life: "I am not ignorant how hard a matter it is to intermeddle with princes' lives, themselves yet being alive; lest, either from flattery a man shall seem to say too much, or saying no more than truth, to say too little" (8:602). In the instance of Elizabeth, Foxe's biographical method is to record and interpret the events of her life so as to pose her in several familiar roles. During her sister's reign, she is held a harsh captive, a poor defenseless girl who, Foxe solemnly relates, would gladly have exchanged her state for that of a poor milkmaid she hears singing outside her prison. Even though imprisoned and threatened, however, she clings to her Protestant principles as devoutly as any of the martyrs and, as a witness to the faith, she is accorded a place in their ranks. This dual portrait of Elizabeth, as defenseless woman requiring the sympathy and support of all men of good will and as steadfast heroine, inspirational and admirable, is writ larger after her accession to the throne. As Francis Yates shows, Foxe presents Elizabeth the queen in the role of imperial monarch, as a second Constantine divinely appointed to restore purity and prestige to a besieged land and faith.[22] Even as Foxe casts Elizabeth as imperial monarch, embodiment of the combined moral force and national spirit of Protestant England, the lonely girl in her sister's dungeon, sighing to be a milkmaid, lives on in Foxe's pages; even after she becomes queen, Foxe's Elizabeth is still a single woman beset on every side by enemies and sustained only by the grace of God and the total devotion and allegiance of her people. Thus, through the adroit manipulation of the facts of Elizabeth's life, Foxe fits her personal experience into preexistent roles familiar to and popular with Englishmen. Early in her reign Foxe constructs the twin pillars of the Virgin Queen's great personal popularity and lays the foundation for her apotheosis by a succeeding generation of writers. As a weak, persecuted woman, she requires their support and fidelity; as an imperial monarch, she commands their respect and reverence. Foxe's skill as a propagandist of genius is perhaps nowhere better seen than in his biographical presentation of Elizabeth in the roles of poor milkmaid and imperial monarch.

Foxe's biographical strategy for minor characters in his narrative combines the same elements as his strategy for major figures, but in an inverse manner of presentation. The major figures, Cromwell, Latimer, Winchester, and the rest, are introduced as idiosyncratic individuals, their portraits freighted with factual detail, who gradually come to be perceived as types, as the good shepherd or the ravenous wolf. The minor characters, however, are usually introduced as types, with little more identifying information than the fact that they are papal agents or poor Christian yeomen. As has often been remarked, Foxe's genius in the presentation of these figures is to bring them alive, to authenticate them as unique individuals, through his talent for sharp description, his eye for distinguishing, dramatic detail, and his splendid ear for dialogue. In his treatment of minor figures, such as Kerby of Ipswich who comes to the stake in his nightcap as secure and ready to sleep in the flames as in his own bed, Foxe moves down the scale of abstraction from type to individual. Nevertheless, a narrative formula is clearly apparent in Foxe's treatment of the martyrs whose stories comprise the bulk of his book.

The Structure and Style of Foxe's Biographies

The typical martyr's story Foxe arranges in three relatively distinct segments, each with a climax of its own. The first movement of the stories, as related either by Foxe's narrative or in testimonials written by the martyrs themselves and printed by Foxe, involves the martyr's initial conflict with the authorities, his apprehension, and the physical oppression or torture. Here are exciting stories of honest men and women standing up in churches and public places to rebuke an errant clergy and to refuse a false ritual, reaffirming the true Protestant faith. Next comes a suspenseful narrative of house-to-house searches, paid informers, hair-breadth escapes, and the inevitable apprehension, followed by vivid descriptions of torture and abuse. The emphasis in this first stage of the martyr's story is on physical action, the thrill of the martyr taking a public stand against evil, the suspense of the chase as the authorities hunt him down, and the pathetic account of the whippings, stocking, and the like abuse by which the authorities hope to conquer the will by breaking the body. The focus here is on heroic action and physical endurance, climaxing in the martyr's triumph over torture.

The second stage derives from the success of the first. Having taken a public stand and resisted the temptation to give way under physical suffering, the martyr is examined on the grounds of his belief by a clerical court or committee made up of the bishop of his diocese and various other inquisitors drawn from the ranks of the clergy. Here the emphasis is on doctrine rather than action and the conflict is a test of faith rather than nerve and stamina, the weapons now words. The martyr was required to define and defend his faith under skilled cross-examination by a group of clergy with far better education and full access to research materials, commentaries, books, and tracts denied the martyr. To the pride and delight of generations of English readers, in Foxe's pages David regularly slew Goliath in these encounters, as the martyrs stood resolutely by a plain asseveration of their faith based upon the Bible, rejecting the arguments of the clergy and often mounting effective counterattacks upon the mass, papal supremacy, and other Catholic doctrines. In these examinations, the dramatic presentation of the martyr's steadfast spirit and faith under assault produces a powerful rhetorical climax, often set forth in the martyr's own words, which explains and validates the active heroism of the first stage.

The final scene at the stake completes and justifies the three-stage pattern. The action and suspense of the first stage are reflected in the manner of death of the martyr. Would the martyr die well, as an exemplum of the *ars moriendi Christiani,* or would the frailty of the flesh and the sight of the flames lead to a terrified recantation or a screaming, ghastly death in the inferno? Or would he succumb to the promises and lures of his tormentors to buy his life, perhaps even his freedom, by abjuring his faith even before the fire was put to him? Here, in the death scenes described by Foxe and sketched by his engravers, heroic action and spirit fuse in the indelible portraits of English men and women of every rank and occupation triumphing in the flames over their persecutors. So powerful is Foxe's description of the final scenes that the words, gestures, and prophesies of these Protestant martyrs at the stake became an almost instantaneous part of English folklore, conditioning the response and shaping the attitude even today of most readers toward the Marian period.

These three stages represent the full biographical pattern for the presentation of the minor figures in the *Acts and Monuments*; obviously, the stories of some figures emphasize one or two sections at the expense of the others, but even an abbreviated pattern can excite and move the reader. For example, William Coberley, a tailor martyred at Salisbury in 1556, is a minor figure who receives only a page or so in Foxe's record. Even then he is grouped with two of his companions, a freemason and a husbandman, who encouraged him to accompany them to their parish church to urge their fellowmen of the district to leave worshiping the idol of the mass and "return to the living God" (8:103). Foxe briefly records the arrest, examinations (where the husbandman told the chancellor of Salisbury that "wooden images were good to roast a shoulder of mutton, but evil in the church" [8:104]), and execution of the trio. Coberley's wife, arrested with him, revoked her faith for fear of the fire, but the image of Coberley's difficult but noble death creates an impression of silent heroism which both individualizes and memorializes the nearly anonymous tailor who, Foxe writes, "was somewhat long a burning as the wind stood: after his body was scorched with the fire, and left arm drawn and taken from him by the violence of the fire, the flesh being burnt to the white bone, at length he stooped over the chain, and with the right hand, being some what starkened, knocked upon his breast softly, the blood and matter issuing out of his mouth. Afterward, when they all thought he had been dead, suddenly he rose right up with his body again. And thus much concerning these three Salisbury martyrs" (8:105). The sharp, clinically detailed description of Coberley's terrible death, a death he could have avoided as easily as had his wife, distinguishes and emphasizes his heroism more effectively than any amount of lamentation or apotheosis Foxe might have appended. Hence without rhetorical embroidery, Foxe restores him, after the vivid description of his death, to the company of his fellow Salisbury yeomen in the final laconic sentence of the story.

As the example of William Coberley illustrates, the success of Foxe's biographical strategy is dependent not only upon design but upon style. Aside from a general recognition that individual scenes are enormously moving, however, there is little critical consensus on the quality of Foxe's prose style. For Helen C. White, "Foxe is always swift, vigorous, resonant. There is nothing delicate, nothing elusive, nothing cloudy about his style."[23] Hardin Craig concurs, observing that "the excellence of Foxe's homely prose as well as his skill in the reproduction of vivid dialogue has not been widely recognized by historians of literature, but is attested by centuries of genuine popularity."[24] On the other hand, C. S. Lewis's examination of the *Acts and Monuments* leads to the conclusion that "his English style has no high merits. The sentences have not energy to support their great length."[25] George Williamson is harsher still in his declaration that "Foxe himself was no stylist. . . . Quite apart from irrelevant details and unwanted comments Foxe's writing is full of tautologies and pleonasms."[26] Obviously, out of thousands of pages of the *Acts and Monuments*, selected examples might be found to support the opinion of either camp.[27] Those who deplore excessive looseness and excessiveness, or pleonasm, in Foxe can cite especially his lengthy discussion of the mass and various theological positions as examples of copiousness wrung dry or as digressions and asides, as in this assurance of a divine judgment: "But at length it shall appear, and peradventure sooner than shall be expedient for some, except with speedy repentance they do wax wise and amend, which, that it may the better be brought to pass, suffer me a little by your license, gentle reader, to talk with these cruel bloodsuckers; whereby they, being admonished, may repent; or if they will not, that they may behold, to their great shame and rebuke, whether they will or no, their wicked cruelty and great slaughters, laid before them, as it were upon a stage" (3:98).

Almost any of the dialogue reported in the *Acts and Monuments* illustrates the force and clarity Foxe could command; indeed, even in descriptive portions he can marshal a concatenation of phrases and clauses to drive home a point with powerful subtlety. In relating the case of a poor painter of Colchester, confined in the bishop's house as a heretic after he painted some Scripture verses on cloths designed to hang in the new Colchester Inn, Foxe describes in a single sentence a casual atrocity of the sort the times bred: "His wife, in the time of the suit, while he was yet at Fulham, being desirous to see her husband, and pressing to come in at the gate, being then great with child, the porter lifted up his foot and struck her on the body, that at length she died of the same; but the child was destroyed immediately" (4:695). Foxe neither comments upon nor embellishes this terrible incident; rather his syntax heightens the horror, the leisurely phrases of the first portion yielding to the stark clauses of its conclusion. There are no adjectives or adverbs in the sentence; rather the shape of the period is decisive, as the reader first learns of the wife's condition, then of the atrocity itself and its consequence for the woman. First the reader learns that she eventually died of the assault; only then, in the final member of the sentence, does he learn that the child died instantly. By suspending this information until the close of the sentence, Foxe forces the reader to reevaluate an already painful story. No sooner has the reader sympathetically dismissed her to a martyr's death than he is told another soul died in her and is left to reflect on the additional agony, mental and physical, which the death of the fetus must have caused the poor woman. In such sentences, spare, compact, and distinguished by highly functional syntax, Foxe is an impressive prose craftsman.

As the examples suggest, Foxe's style is not uniform throughout the *Acts and Monuments*; in a work so long, composed over a period of decades, it would be surprising if there were no unevenness. The mark Foxe set for himself, however, as his stylistic goal is clear: a direct and plain style built upon factual declaration. He has no use for the spidery distinctions of the Schoolmen and no time for the polished periods of Cicero. To those who seek other virtues than plainness and factual accuracy in his writing, Foxe's retort to the strictures of Nicholas Harpsfield, writing under the pseudonym Alan Cope, must suffice: "I should have taken more leisure and done it better. I grant and confess my fault; such is my vice, I cannot sit all the day, Master Cope, fining and mincing my letters, and combing my head, and smoothing my self all the day at the glass of Cicero; yet, notwithstanding, doing what I can, and doing my good will, me thinks I should not be reprehended" (3:384). Foxe viewed his style as an imitation of the apostles', a plain vehicle for plain truth; thus, he quotes with apparent favor the distinctive differences between true and false prophets set forth in *De Periculis Ecclesiae*: "The apostles study neither for eloquence, nor for the curious placing of their words, but false prophets do both as [1 Cor. 14:23], 'If the simple and ineloquent man,' etc. Glossa:—'The apostles were not eloquent but false prophets are full of curious eloquence.' Also upon the same subject from another gloss: 'The Corinthians were led away from the gospel by over nice eloquence' [2 Cor. 6:4]" (2:514). Indeed, Foxe frequently calls cautionary attention to the slippery rhetoric of the forces of Antichrist, as in his prefatory comment to a letter of Pope Adrian VI to the German princes stirring them against Martin Luther: "I thought therefore to give the reader a sight thereof, to the intent that by the experience of them he may learn hereafter, in cases like, to be prudent and circumspect in believing over-rashly the smooth talk or pretensed persuasions of men, especially in church-matters, unless they carry with them the simplicity of plain truth; going not upon terms, but grounded upon the word and revealed will of God, with particular demonstrations, proving that by the Scripture which they pretend to persuade" (4:295). Thus, for Foxe, the plain style was the only fit one for his honest gospel truth.

As every reader of the *Acts and Monuments* knows, Foxe often evaded or ignored his theoretical commitment to a plain, denotative style. While he could use effectively an unadorned style, often through haste or design he did not; thus, Foxe is neither a neo-Senecan nor a proto-Augustan prose stylist. While syntax varies a great deal from one portion of the *Acts and Monuments* to another, there are several characteristic features of Foxe's style which deserve notice as contributing factors in the success of the work. A passage from Foxe's dedication to Queen Elizabeth commenting on the hostile reception the 1563 edition received among Catholics will illustrate several of the prominent features of Foxe's style:

Not that there were in it such lies in very deed, but that the coming of that book should not betray their lying falsehood, therefore they thought best to begin first to make exceptions themselves against it; playing in their stage like as Phormio did in the old comedy, who, being in all the fault himself, began first to quarrel with Demipho, when Demipho rather had good right to lay Phormio by the heels.

With like facing brags these catholic Phormiones think now to dash out all good books, and, amongst others also, these Monuments of Martyrs: which godly martyrs as they could not abide being alive, so neither can they now suffer their memories to live after their death, lest the acts of them, being known, might bring perhaps their wicked acts and cruel murders to detestation; and therefore spurn they so vehemently against this book of histories, with all kind of contumelies and uproars, railing and wondering upon it. Much like as I have heard of a company of thieves, who in robbing a certain true man by the highway side, when they had found a piece of gold or two about him more than he would be known of, they cried out of the falsehood of the world, marvelling and complaining what little truth was to be found in men. Even so these men deal also with me; for when they themselves altogether delight in untruths, and have replenished the whole church of Christ with feigned fables, lying miracles, false visions, and miserable errors, contained in their missals, portuses, breviaries, and summaries, and almost no true tale in all their saints' lives and festivals, as now also no great truths in our Louvanian books, etc.; yet notwithstanding, as though they were a people of much truth, and that the world did not perceive them, they pretend a face and zeal of great verity; and as though there were no histories else in all the world corrupted, but only this History of Acts and Monuments, with tragical voices they exclaim and wonder upon it, sparing no cost of hyperbolical phrases to make it appear as full of lies as lines, etc. (1:vii)

This passage illustrates the texture of Foxe's prose through the layers of allusion he uses to clarify his points and support his case. First, the reference to Terence's characters is a fair sample of the thread of classical allusion woven through the *Acts and Monuments*. Foxe had read the Greek and Latin classics in his schooldays and he draws examples from them freely to entertain and instruct the more learned class of readers who would recognize the allusions. Among the classical authors, his favorites (setting aside Eusebius and the historians) seem to be the dramatists, and consequently the *Acts and Monuments* is peppered with references especially to the plays of Plautus and Terence. Foxe was himself the author of Latin plays, including the "apocalyptic comedy" *Christus Triumphans,* and the frequency of his allusions to the Roman comic dramatists may reflect his special study of them or his confidence that, as staples of the Elizabethan grammar school curriculum, his readers would recognize them more readily than references to other classical texts. The allusions to classical comedy support another feature of Foxe's style found in this passage and throughout the *Acts and Monuments:* the use of metaphors drawn from the stage. Here the Catholics are portrayed as bad actors, their "tragical voices" hollow and unconvincing. These stage metaphors are so frequent (e.g., Latimer and Ridley both treat and describe the disputations at Oxford as a farce, an interlude, and the like, while Foxe describes Latimer's makeup and appearance, as a semisenile old preacher, in theatrical terms; the burning of the martyrs is repeatedly described in the language of the theater, as the martyrs try to win over the audience by their behavior at the stake, while Foxe calls the exhumation and burning of martyrs' bones by Cardinal Pole a pageant and interlude) that they ultimately suggest a way of looking at history as pageant, with the author instructing the reader especially on how to recognize a good performance and appreciate the continuity of theme through changes of scene and cast. Thus, in the dark ages when Satan was unloosed, "so up started a new sort of players, to furnish the stage, as school-doctors, canonists, and four orders of friars"(1:xxi), a cast of villains who plagued England until the time of Henry VIII and his son Edward VI when, Foxe writes, "a new face of things began now to appear, as it were on a stage, new players coming in, the old being thrust out; for the most part the bishops of churches and dioceses were changed: such as had been dumb prelates before, were then compelled to give place to others then, that would preach and take pains" (5:703). Thus Foxe announces the conclusion of the dumb show and the opening of the play proper. So by the Marian reversion which follows, Foxe has set the stage and taught his readers how to react as proper spectators to the grimmest and most glorious tragedies.

While the layer of classical allusions embellishes Foxe's scholarship and enriches the work especially for the more learned reader, the familiar anecdote, often of a witty nature such as the story of the indignant thieves, possesses an unrestricted appeal. The anecdotal habit in Foxe's composition, explaining, illustrating, and clarifying through example and allusion, is a vital ingredient of his style. This and his humor prevent the narrative from descending to dry recitation. The range of Foxe's humor is particularly noteworthy. There are complete comic stories, such as that of the imagined fire at Cambridge which panicked the solemn scholars into most indecorous behavior; comic characters, such as the dancing preacher old Hubberdin or Justice Nine-Holes; mockery and parody, as in Foxe's reconstruction of "the deep divinity of our Catholic masters" (1:108) arguing over whether St. Mary had a confessor, if so who and what she had to confess; irony, as in Foxe's notice that medieval chronicles report Edward III did "offer in the church of Westminster the vestments where in St. Peter did celebrate mass; which belike were well kept from moths to last so long" (2:722); puns, as in his comment on papal tributes during the Middle Ages as "some new invention from Rome to fetch in our English money; and if all the floods in England (yea in all Europe) did run not into the sea of Rome, yet were that ocean never able to be satisfied" (3:772); and direct comic derision, as in his laconic scolia upon the power of Catholic bishops to free souls from purgatory and facilitate their passage to heaven: "Like a pulled hen" (3:164).

In a consideration of the texture of Foxe's prose, however, there is another vital level of allusion not present in the representative passage cited which must be noticed: biblical allusions. The Scriptures are the one text everyone in Foxe's audience knew, and his allusions to biblical people and events are more frequent than either classical references or homely anecdotes and illustrations. Often, the biblical allusion accompanies some other reference, as in Foxe's regret that England did not follow the example of the Greek church in renouncing Roman Catholicism early: "But such was the rude dulnes then of miserable Englãd, for lacke of learnyng and godly knowledge, that they feling what burdens were layd upon them, yet would play still ye asse of Balaam, or els the horse of Esope, which receiuyng the bridle once in hys mouth, could afterward neither abide hys owne misery, nor yet recouer libertie. And so it fared with England under the Popes thraldome. . . ."[28] The biblical allusions are so extensive that, like the allusions to drama and the stage, they persistently suggest another way of viewing the histories of the *Acts and Monuments:* as the recurrent fulfillment of prophesies and types set forth in the Scriptures. The analogical habit of Scriptural reference is so deeply engrained that Foxe turns to it almost automatically, as in his warning to Catholic inquisitors to "let these men take heed that while they go about, by their own fantasies rather than by any just judgment, to put heretics to death, that the same things do not happen unto them which in times past happened unto the Jews, who when they would have entered upon Christ as a seditious man, they stumbled upon the Son of God" (3:104). Here temporary and local persecution of Lollards by the English Catholic hierarchy is placed in truer frame of reference by the reminder that the persecution of Protestant yeomen by English bishops is part of an action begun by the persecution of a Nazarene carpenter by Pontius Pilate and the Sanhedrin. Thus the biblical analogy is a constant reminder that a chronological recounting of the sequence of the years is but one way of viewing history; a truer recounting may be to fit all human history into the timeless conflict between Good and Evil set forth in the Bible and continuing until the Second Coming. And, as noted in the discussion of biographical strategy in the *Acts and Monuments,* Foxe makes extensive use of the biographical parallel in comparing historical figures to biblical ones, as in the wealth of allusions and comparisons of Edward VI to the young Israelite king Josias of the Old Testament. And casual comparisons of historical figures to biblical ones are everywhere in the *Acts and Monuments,* as in Foxe's comments upon Henry Philips, who betrayed William Tyndale to the Catholic authorities after pretending to be his friend: "That traitor, worse than Judas to man's judgment in the act doing, only not comparing to Christ, and that the Scriptures hath already judged Judas, otherwise not so good; for Judas, after he had betrayed his Master and Friend, was sorry, acknowledged and confessed his fact openly, declared his Master to be the very Truth, despising the money that he had received for doing the act, brought it again and cast it before them. This traitor Philips, contrariwise, not lamenting, but rejoicing in that he had done, not declaring the honest goodness and truth of his friend, but applied, in all that he could devise, to declare him to be false and seditious. . . ." (5:128). In sum, the various levels of allusion in the *Acts and Monuments* add a density and a texture even to the plain, straightforward factual record Foxe professes to write, supplying depth and additional dimensions to his narrative history.

Foxe as Controversialist

One area in which Foxe apparently had particular difficulty in maintaining a level style and fit decorum was that of controversy and personal attack. Foxe was adept at flyting, a familiar recourse in theological controversy of the sixteenth century, and he required an effort of will to resist. Thus when Harpsfield attacked him under the pseudonym of Cope, Foxe's reply begins to slip into a name-calling match. Painfully, he pulls himself up short:

But now like a spider-catcher, sucking out of every one what is the worst, to make up your laystall, you heap up a dung-hill of dirty dialogues, containing nothing in them but malicious railing, virulent slanders, manifest untruths, opprobrious contumelies, and stinking blasphemies, able almost to corrupt and infect the air. Such is the malady and 'cacoethes' of your pen, that it beginneth to bark, before it hath learned well to write, which pen of yours, notwithstanding, I do not here reproach or condemn, as neither do I greatly fear the same. God, of his mercy, keep the SWORD out of the papists' hand: it is not the PEN of the papists I greatly pass upon, though twenty Copes and so many surplices were set against the 'Book of Monuments,' were I so disposed, Master Cope, to dally . . . and to repay again as I am provoked. But, in despiteful railing, and in this satirical sort of barking, I give you over. . . . Mildness and humanity rather beseemeth, and is the grace of the Latin phrase. (3:372)

Notable here are two tendencies characteristic of Foxe's attack upon adversaries throughout the *Acts and Monuments:* a recourse to *ad hominem* attack and a fondness for caricaturing opponents as beasts, as Cope is here first a spider and then a dog. While Foxe generally checks these tendencies before they get out of hand, excesses occur, as in his slander of St. Francis of Assisi, singled out in Foxe's record for "maintaining blind hypocrisy" (2:263). Foxe's denigration of St. Francis is unusually vicious:

This Assisian ass, who I suppose was some simple and rude idiot, hearing, upon a time, how Christ sent forth his disciples to preach, thought to imitate the same in himself and his disciples, and so left off his shoes; he had but one coat, and that of coarse cloth. . . . He left in writing, to his disciples and followers, his rule, which he called "Regulam Evangelicam," the rule of the gospel. As though the gospel of Christ were not a sufficient rule to all Christian men, but it must take its perfection of frantic Francis. (2:351)

The tendency to caricature his adversaries as ravening wolves and the like, already noticed in Foxe's description of Bishop Bonner, occasionally erupts into such florid excess as his description of the challenge by a stout papist to the Protestant Scots preacher, George Wisehart: "When that this fed sow had read throughout all his lying menacings, his face running down with sweat, and frothing at the mouth like a boar, he spit at Master George's face, saying, 'What answereth thou to these sayings, thou runnagate! traitor! thief! which we have duly proved by sufficient witness against thee?'" (5:628). In the ensuing exchange, Foxe continues the caricature by repeatedly depicting the papist as "the fed sow . . . with hoggist voice." It is true, as Richard S. Sylvester suggests, that Foxe toned down some of the most inflammatory rhetoric of the 1563 edition in subsequent revisions.[29] For example, "The greedy and insatiable tyranny of the most cruel papists, and, rather, bloody horse-leeches; I mean Bonner and his complices," of 1563 is rephrased in subsequent editions as "note the unreasonable, or rather unnatural doing of these unmerciful Catholics (I mean bishop Bonner and his complices), in whom was so little mercy to all sorts and kinds of men, that also they spared neither impotent age, neither lame nor blind, as may well appear . . ." (8:140). Although the entire area of Foxe's stylistic revisions in the various editions of the *Acts and Monuments* has been largely neglected by critics, Sylvester's point that the rhetoric of the 1563 edition is a good deal more inflammatory than that of the later editions seems sound.

While it is true, then, that Foxe moderates his rhetoric to some extent in the editions of the 1570s, he does not attentuate his descriptions or seek to spare the reader the full emotional impact of the deaths of the martyrs. For example, one of the most horrible atrocities in Foxe's bloody record is the infamous story of the burning of three women, a mother and her two grown daughters, on the island of Guernsey in 1556 (8:226–33). Foxe describes how one of the daughters went into labor in the flames and was delivered of a male child, who was plucked from the fire by a bystander and taken to the provost and bailiff. These officials pronounced the child no less tainted with heresy than its mother; consequently, the child was returned to the fire where it was consumed with its mother, grandmother, and aunt. This terrible story was attacked by Thomas Harding in his *Rejoinder* to Bishop Jewel of 1567, who argues the women were lawfully condemned as thieves and strumpets as well as heretics. Rather than altering his account of the incident, Foxe appended to his account in the text of 1570 "A Defence of This Guernsey Story Against Master Harding" citing supplemental witnesses, depositions, and other supporting evidence. In turn, this mass of affidavits, official reports, and other data in a flat, declarative prose sets off and intensifies Foxe's original description of the atrocity.[30]

The sensational Guernsey incident bears out the truth of Helen C. White's assertion that "Foxe has a genius for the full sensuous presentation of a situation that will bring it to life in the reader's imagination with a vitality that will make it an ineradicable part of his consciousness."[31] In lieu of authorial comment on the terrible spectacles he describes, Foxe prefers to present them, as White observes, with a palpability and a clinical accuracy whose vividness is so moving that commentary is superfluous. The description itself may be counted upon to evoke the emotional recoil at which Foxe aims. Many of the burnings of English martyrs were particularly agonizing, due to the dampness of the climate and the indifference of the authorities toward building a large, quick fire, and Foxe's descriptions of prolonged sufferings of such martyrs as Nicholas Ridley have been cited earlier. Foxe's account of the death of Bishop John Hooper in 1555 at Gloucester illustrates the rhetorical power of the minute, sensuous description of horrible deeds. Hooper had requested of the sheriffs "only, that there may be a quick fire, shortly to make an end" (6:655), and assisted by his friends, he came to the stake where "being in his shirt, he took a point from his hose himself, and trussed his shirt between his legs, where he had a pound of gunpowder in a bladder, and under each arm the like quantity, delivered him by the guard" (6:657). All his hopes and precautions for a speedy death were frustrated, however, as Foxe describes in agonizing detail, as three fires are kindled in an attempt to dispatch Hooper properly:

Within a space after, a few dry faggots were brought, and a new fire kindled with faggots (for there were no more reeds), and that burned at the nether parts, but had small power above, because of the wind, saving that it did burn his hair, and scorch his skin a little. In the time of which fire, even as at the first flame, he prayed, saying mildly and not very loud (but as one without pains), "O Jesus, the Son of David, have mercy upon me, and receive my soul!" After the second was spent, he did wipe both his eyes with his hands, and beholding the people, he said with an indifferent loud voice, "For God's love, good people, let me have more fire!" And all this while his nether parts did burn: for the faggots were so few, that the flame did not burn strongly at his upper parts.

The third fire was kindled within a while after, which was more extreme than the other two: and then the bladders of gunpowder brake, which did him small good, they were so placed, and the wind had such power. In the which fire he prayed with somewhat a loud voice, "Lord Jesus, have mercy upon me; Lord Jesus, have mercy upon me: Lord Jesus, receive my spirit!" And these were the last words he was heard to utter. But when he was black in the mouth, and his tongue swollen, that he could not speak, yet his lips went till they were shrunk to the gums: and he knocked his breast with his hands,

until one of his arms fell off, and then knocked still with the other, what time
the fat, water, and blood, dropped out at his fingers' ends, until by renewing
of the fire his strength was gone, and his hand did cleave fast, in knocking to
the iron upon his breast. So immediately, bowing forwards, he yielded up his
spirit. . . . Thus was he three quarters of an hour or more in the fire. Even as
a lamb, patiently he abode the extremity thereof, neither moving forwards,
backwards, nor to any side: but, having his nether parts burned, and his
bowels fallen out, he died as quietly as a child in his bed. (6:658–59)

Commentary can add little to the impact of such a description, augmented by an engraving of Hooper in the flames, and Foxe elects to
allow the incandescent horror of his verbal portrait to work upon the
reader without pointing or exclamation from the author.

This preference for the descriptive over the hortatory mode is a
conscious artistic one in Foxe's case; on other occasions, he thrusts
himself so forcefully into his text as to become almost an actor himself
in the great events he describes. Through the development of a distinct
authorial voice and stance, Foxe maintains the essential distinction
between documented fact and authorial commentary. But here the
personal and emotive is given scope; Foxe's reactions and comments are
those of a committed, caring Christian to the events of history. These
comments are designed not to dupe the reader (since they are clearly
labeled as authorial reactions) but to move him. In brief, the ethical
dimension in the *Acts and Monuments* is another attempt to resolve the
tension between Foxe as an historian committed both to accurate
recording of documented fact and to promulgation of a specifically
Protestant interpretation of history. The character of the author is
another device through which the reader may be won to a right view of
history. The voices of the author vary, from the blunt, often sardonic
scoliast cutting through clouds of verbiage and thickets of scholastic
intricacy to sum up a point in pithy, colloquial marginal comments to
the helpful Protestant historian, pointing out what *should* have occurred rather than settling for the historian's "bare *was*," in Sidney's
phrase. Thus, in this latter capacity, Foxe records the capitulation of
Richard II to the clergy's request for acts of persecution against heretics;
but he also inserts in his text the reply Richard *should have* sent refusing
their request. This imaginary epistle is clearly labeled in the margin as a
"Prosopopoeia. What the king might have answered again" (3:48); it

represents one type of compromise between the two sorts of historical writing Foxe was attempting to straddle.

This technique of thrusting himself into history ultimately goes beyond merely sketching out alternative lines of argument as in the imaginary letter of Richard II. In discussing the condemnation of John Lambert in 1538, a sentence acquiesced to by Henry VIII, Foxe becomes so upset at the persecution of Christians by a Christian monarch that he halts his narrative for a lecture from the Christian historian to Henry VIII, "if that I may a little talk with thee, where-soever thou art" (5:235), on the duty of a monarch to protect, not persecute, truth. In a similar vein, Foxe himself steps in to answer the arguments for the maintenance of Catholicism set forth in Winchester's letters to Protector Somerset during Edward VI's reign. He first prints Winchester's letters, then inserts a section in the text entitled "Certain Additions After These Letters Above Specified, with Notes and Solutions Answering to the Same," where Foxe himself undertakes to refute Winchester. Thus, to Winchester's warning to Somerset to eschew innovation in religion, Foxe retorts that "Foreasmuch therefore as in this alteration there is no new religion brought in, but only the old religion of the primitive church revived; therefore here is to be thought not so much a innovation, as a renovation or reformation rather of religion, which reformation is ofttimes so necessary in commonweals, that, without the same, all runneth to confusion" (6:56–57). Likewise, Foxe heavily glosses Winchester's polemical letters, as in his letter to Ridley defending images. Here Winchester's text receives two thirds of the page while the author, Foxe, argues against Winchester's position through notes and glosses that fill out the page. In such cases, Foxe is almost an historical figure himself, stepping into his own book to combat a departed adversary with ideological weapons.[32]

Here is undisguised partisan history, but without misrepresentation of historical fact. The authorial voice is always there, laconic in the scolia, helpfully pointing and interpreting in the text, morally and emotionally engaged even to set-piece commentaries on the developments of history, always available as a guide for the Protestant reader through a brazen world of mere fact. This authorial voice encourages the confidence and even dependence of the reader, at times sharing

Foxe's own bewilderment at the challenge of history with his readers. For example, in a dramatic passage near the end of the first book of the *Acts and Monuments,* Foxe recalls his perturbation of spirit at the contemplation of the terrible persecutions of Christians under the Roman emperors:

The further I proceeded in the story, and the hotter the persecutions grew, the more my grief with them and for them increased; not only pitying their woful case, but almost reasoning with God, thinking thus like a fool with myself:—why should God of his goodness suffer his children and servants so vehemently to be cruciated and afflicted? If mortal things were governed by heavenly providence (as must needs be granted), why did the wicked so rage and flourish, and the godly go so to wrack? . . . Only in these persecutions under the beast, I found nothing to satisfy my doubt. For, albeit I read there of forty-two months, of a time, times, and half a time, of one thousand two hundred and threescore days; yet all this by computation coming but to three years and a half, came nothing near the long continuance of these persecutions, which lasted three hundred years. Thus, being vexed and turmoiled in spirit about the reckoning of these numbers and years; it so happened upon a Sunday in the morning, I lying in my bed, and musing about these numbers, suddenly it was answered to my mind, as with a majesty, thus inwardly saying within me; "Thou fool, count these months by sabbaths, as the weeks of Daniel are counted by sabbaths." The Lord I take to witness, thus it was. Whereupon thus being admonished, I began to reckon the forty-two months by sabbaths: first, of months; that would not serve: then by sabbaths of years; wherein I began to feel some probable understanding. . . . Now this one clasp being opened, the other numbers that follow are plain and manifest to the intelligent reader to be understood. (1:289–90)

The drama and excitement of the author's Sunday morning epiphany in this autobiographical passage is another contribution to the authorial *ethos,* the character of the narrator/guide to whom the reader is encouraged to look for explanation and interpretation of hard fact. The successful employment of this persona, scrupulous and accurate in his respect for fact, caring and committed to Christian education in his concern for the reader, is a key feature in the widespread acceptance of the *Acts and Monuments* in Protestant England.

Conclusion

In summary, Foxe designed the *Acts and Monuments* to exert a broad and deep appeal to his countrymen. While the work contains within its broad compass a medley of different literary types, the role of the *Acts and Monuments* as a courtesy book teaching not only how to live the Christian life but especially how to die well is fundamental to its appeal to all classes. Indeed, due to the varied facets of the work's visual appeal, even the illiterate members of Foxe's audience could enjoy and learn from it. The engravings are an instance of the repetition of key themes basic to Foxe's narrative strategy. In particular, a study of the composition and presentation of major and minor figures in the history illustrates how Foxe moves from individual to type and back again, playing background against foreground to underscore central themes. The various devices, such as the use of the biographical parallel, the tactical use of realistic surface detail, or the transformation of major characters into moral types, through which the author seeks to satisfy the demands of both scientific and Protestant historical writing, illustrate the craftsmanship of Foxe the artist. Similarly, a study of Foxe's prose style finds it to be remarkably plastic, capable of a variety of effects. In particular, the texture built up of layers of allusion and a fondness for metaphor supports the text by suggesting ways of perceiving history other than as flat chronological record. Thus, if Foxe's prose is not always and everywhere the plain factual record of his ideal, it is nevertheless far more than a shapeless hodgepodge of floating phrases and clauses. Finally, Foxe's spare, clinically detailed descriptions of the martyrs' death scenes taken in conjunction with his manipulation of authorial stance and voice to educate and move the reader are another instance of his attempts to satisfy two different kinds of historical writing. Foxe's passion and commitment have never been doubted; since the vindication of his factual accuracy during the past generation, perhaps the time is right for a full reassessment of the artistry and achievement of the *Acts and Monuments*.

Chapter Four
Miscellaneous Works: Playwright, Preacher, Pastor

Foxe as Dramatist

While Foxe's great book overshadowed, in his own day as for posterity, his other literary productions, several other areas of his literary endeavor produced work of both historical interest and literary merit. Much of his writing and translating was service work: introductions and translations of the works of continental Reformers, for example, and various polemical contributions to the literature of Reformation controversy, often commissioned by members of the Anglican hierarchy. For the most part, these service and polemical works are of interest only to students of Reformation history. As an academic dramatist, a popular preacher, and an author of pastoral rather than theological tracts, however, Foxe composed a body of work which would have secured him a modest niche in the literary history of the English Renaissance even had he not written the *Acts and Monuments*.

Foxe's son Simeon spoke in his memoir of "divers *Latine* Comedies yet to be seen" written by his father while a fellow at Magdalen College in the 1540s.[1] Only two of Foxe's Latin comedies survive, and one of these appears to date not from his Oxford years but from a decade later when he was in exile abroad. Although the two plays are both academic Latin comedies laced with characters, devices, and verbal echoes of Plautus and Terence, they are actually quite dissimilar productions. Brought together in a modern edition and translation by John Hazel Smith, paradoxically these two plays are today the most accessible works in the Foxe canon—and the only ones available in a modern scholarly edition.

Titus et Gesippus is the sole survivor of Foxe's Oxford comedies; a single, heavily edited manuscript copy, presumably Foxe's foul papers, exists in the Lansdowne collection of Foxe papers in the British Library. Foxe sent copies of the play to two friends, apparently as a demonstration of his competence to teach Latin, in early 1545 when he had determined to leave Oxford and seek a tutorial post. In his letters accompanying the copies, Foxe notes that he wrote the play during the previous autumn and hopes to revise it; these presentation copies are lost and the surviving manuscript is presumably an early version.[2] The play was not published until Smith's modern edition, and although there was a good deal of dramatic activity at Magdalen during the 1540s, there is no evidence to indicate whether or not the play was acted there or elsewhere. Nevertheless, the very existence of a romantic comedy from the pen of Foxe, even if written as an academic exercise, suggests another facet of his character, one at odds with the modern perception of him as a sober moralist and ecclesiastical historian.

The plot of *Titus et Gesippus,* the story of two exemplary friends, ultimately derives from one of the tales in Boccaccio's *Decameron,* although Foxe seems to have followed a version found in Sir Thomas Elyot's *Book of the Governour.* Foxe's play is one of the earliest English dramatic treatments of a favorite Renaissance theme, the conflict between Friendship and Love, the subject a generation later of Lyly's *Euphues,* Shakespeare's *Two Gentlemen of Verona,* and a host of other literary works. In Foxe's play, Gesippus, a noble Athenian youth, celebrates the advent of his nuptial day as his father concludes arrangements of his dowry and prepares a feast to follow the marriage.

Unknown to him, his best friend Titus, a Roman youth, is languishing of love melancholy for Sempronia, Gesippus's bride-to-be, a secret Titus confides to his clever slave, Phormio. After devising a plan based on the remarkable physical similarity of the two youths, Phormio confronts Gesippus with a proposal to save Titus's life by allowing his friend to take his place at the wedding and marry Sempronia. In accord with the fashionable Renaissance exaltation of friendship, Gesippus makes the correct choice:

Anyone who professes to be a friend in good times should prove that he is one in difficult times as well. Though I certainly can't deny that I love her too, I don't love her so much that I would not readily put my friend ahead of everything, even if it meant losing my life, which is dearer to me than she is. So don't think the loss of a girl is of such importance to me. If he is so smitten with love that he must die without her, I am not such a scoundrel, Phormio, that I would ever allow his safety to be locked up in a prison of my joys. He must have her. (*L,* 95)

The marriage switch works, followed by Titus's return to Rome with Sempronia.

When Gesippus's father learns what has happened, he banishes his son, who also departs, in penury, for Rome. Upon Gesippus's arrival, Titus and Sempronia do not recognize him in his rags and, despairing, he contemplates suicide but instead falls asleep by the public road. There he is found sleeping by a desperado, Martius, who has robbed and wounded a local farmer. Martius places his bloody dagger in Gesippus's hand and rouses the countryside against Gesippus. A listless and uncaring Gesippus then appears to confess the crime and is taken before the consuls, one of whom is Titus, for examination. Thinking he recognizes his old friend under the rags, Titus postpones the hearing while he ascertains the identity of the defendant. Titus then encounters an Athenian noble bearing a letter from Gesippus's father forgiving him, and he realizes it is his friend in the dock. Meanwhile, Sempronia sends Phormio to sound out Pamphilia, a Roman girl previously admired by Gesippus, about a marriage with the Athenian. The final act presents the trial scene when the women intercede unsuccessfully for Gesippus. To save his friend, Titus then confesses to the crime, thoroughly confusing his fellow consul. Meanwhile Martius, the real criminal, who has been feeling pangs of conscience, is so overwhelmed at this signal proof of true friendship that he steps forward and confesses all. The play ends with a pardon for Martius and a feast of reconciliation crowning the marriage of Gesippus and Pamphilia.

Even in the rough state preserved in the Lansdowne manuscript, the play is an interesting example of Renaissance academic comedy; Smith calls it "an epitome of English Renaissance comedy, but quite an early specimen" (*L,* 9). Foxe has some problems providing convincing motivation for Gesippus's initial grand gesture; he relies very heavily on coincidence to make the plot function; and he reveals a penchant for crowding key decisions into soliloquies rather than allowing them to develop out of the natural interchange of dialogue between characters. Still, some of the dialogue is quite lively, and in the addition of the Terentian witty slave Phormio, who manipulates much of the early action in particular, Foxe gave a new cast to the story he found in Elyot. In presenting a popular moral exemplum on the ideal of friendship in a lively neoclassical comic mode, Foxe's dramatic experiment in *Titus et Gesippus* is on balance a success.

Closer in spirit to Foxe's nondramatic works is his "apocalyptic comedy" *Christus Triumphans*. This play was printed in Basel in March, 1556, by Oporinus, for whom Foxe was working as a proofreader. Foxe dedicated the work to several English merchants living in Frankfort, apparently hoping both to patch up some of the still festering problems in the congregation there and also to secure some financial support for himself. Although T. W. Baldwin suggests the play is a product of Foxe's Oxford years and posits a now lost English edition of the work in 1551,[3] J. F. Mozley denies the evidence for an English edition[4] and J. H. Smith, on the basis of internal evidence, especially a putative allusion to Latimer and Ridley's incarceration in the jail at Oxford in 1554, denies an early date of composition (*L*, 31–33). There is a holograph copy of the play in the Lansdowne papers at the British Library, and in addition to the 1556 printing, an edition of the play was published at Nuremberg in 1590 and a text edition for schools printed in England in 1672 and reprinted in 1676. Foxe's old friend Lawrence Humphrey wrote asking his permission to stage the play at Oxford, but there is no record of a performance there; the play was performed at Trinity College, Cambridge, in 1562–63.

Christus Triumphans is not, as one might expect from the title, a Resurrection play. Instead it is a fascinating mix of elements drawn from chronicle, mystery, morality, and classical dramatic traditions. In his prologue, Foxe writes that "Our matter is totally sacred and totally apocalyptic, what has been heard of by many but never seen before" (*L*, 229). In the admixture of dramatic traditions, conventions, and characters (they range from the historical, like Peter and Paul, to the typical, like Hierologus the preacher, to the allegorical, like Pseudamnus the false lamb), Foxe's play does resemble several earlier Latin plays in the "Christian Terence" tradition, such as Thomas Kirchmeyer's *Pammachius* (1536) to which Foxe's play may be indebted.[5] Structurally, *Christus Triumphans* is a great sprawling play, only loosely divided into acts; Foxe does not even get around to introducing his apparent central character, Ecclesia (the true church), until the third act. As his prologue promises, the plot is rooted in scenes from the book of Revelation, dramatizing the war between the angelic host and the dragon who is cast into hell by the Lamb. Satan retaliates with his creatures the beast and the false lamb persecuting Ecclesia and her children. The Whore of Babylon appears to fornicate with the kings of the earth, and the play ends with the fall of Babylon, the capture of the beast, and the expectation of the imminent Marriage of the Lamb. However, Foxe also includes incidents from the Gospels and Acts as well as a capsule historical sweep through the history of the church from apostolic times to the Reformation similar to that he would work out in detail in the 1570 edition of the *Acts and Monuments*.[6]

A brief summary of the action of *Christus Triumphans* will illustrate the mixture of religious materials woven into it and also indicate how Foxe's apocalyptic view of history is worked out here in dramatic terms on the same model as it would appear in narrative form in the *Acts and Monuments*. The play begins shortly after Christ's crucifixion with, instead of the three Marys, Eve and the Virgin Mary weeping, Eve for her daughter Psyche (the Soul) stolen by Satan, and Mary for Christ. At this point, Satan appears cast down from heaven while Christus Redivivus rescues Psyche from hell and dispatches her to heaven to await her brother Soma (the Flesh). In the second act Satan and his cohorts have triumphed and hold the world captive, although Peter and Paul struggle against them. Ecclesia opens the third act with a lament for her children, Asia, Africus, and Europus, imprisoned by Nomocrates (the Old Testament Law). Peter and Paul aid in the rescue of Ecclesia from the same tyrant and predict the release of her children even as the era of persecution under the Roman emperors begins. Ecclesia's prospects brighten with the coming of Constantine and his successors until the unloosing of Satan from his thousand-year bondage. With his allies Pope Pseudamnus (the false lamb or Antichrist) and Pornapolis (the Whore of Babylon), Ecclesia suffers another fall. Asia is taken by the Turks, and Europus and Africus are seduced by Pornapolis, who outfaces Ecclesia in a confrontation over who really is the true church and sends the poor mother to Bedlam. In the final act, Hierologus (the preacher/prophet) appears to warn Europus of his deception, denounce Satan's henchmen, and signal the onset of the Reformation; thus Pornapolis laments to Pseudamnus on the turning tide: "You ask if I've heard, when we're already a common story on everybody's lips. They're all diligently reading scriptures—stonecutters, smiths, potters, everybody. And, what I think is bad, the dregs of the people are starting to be wise now. What's more, they're even weighing our traditions in the scales of the gospel" (L, 347). The play concludes with a family reunion of Ecclesia and her children Europus and Africus after which the Wise Virgins appear to deck Ecclesia with robes for the Bride of Christ who is anticipated momentarily. A final epithalamion sung by the Chorus of Virgins urges the spectators to prepare themselves and their lives for the Second Coming since all is ready.

Artistically, *Christus Triumphans* is less successful than *Titus et Gesippus*; even J. H. Smith, the play's editor and principal modern apologist, admits the play is "seriously flawed" (L, 37). Foxe attempts too much, his plan is too vast for his dramatic skills, and consequently there are numerous problems of execution. There is a surplus of characters, most of them flat and colorless, and, more disturbing, allegorical equivalents are not always firmly fixed, as in the case of Ecclesia, Pornapolis, and some other central characters whose precise identification seems to shift from scene to scene. The Latin verse is generally undistinguished, and the sudden shifts and grand sweep of the action require a heavy dependence upon messengers to report the doings of off-stage characters.

As a specimen of the development of academic comedy in the sixteenth century, on the other hand, the play is most interesting. Marvin T. Herrick considers it in his discussion of the Christian Terence, the body of Biblical drama incorporating classical principles written especially for the instruction of students,[7] and Ruth H. Blackburn relates it to the tradition of Latin humanist drama exemplified by the plays of Kirchmeyer and John Bale.[8] But it is the very ambitiousness of Foxe's attempt in *Christus Triumphans* that distinguishes it from earlier plays of a similar type. In particular, Foxe's extremely eclectic borrowings from earlier dramatic traditions make *Christus Triumphans* more interesting to historians of Renaissance drama than *Titus et Gesippus*. Along with his indebtedness to the semi-allegorical propaganda plays of Kirchmeyer and Bale, Foxe's portrayal of Ecclesia seduced, buffeted, and comforted by various good and evil characters, along with the allegorical characters and inset nondramatic theological discussions, points to the influence of the medieval morality play.[9] In its free amplification of biblical materials and, as J. H. Smith suggests (*L,* 38), especially in the radical telescoping of time, *Christus Triumphans* betrays an indebtedness to the medieval mystery plays. The attempt to dramatize the events of a 1,500-year period, complete with the appearance of selected historical characters, suggests like Foxe's prologue that the dramatist aimed at a kind of chronicle play. And in the five-act division, the extensive use of a messenger to report off-stage action, and the employment of the language of Roman comedy throughout, Foxe's debt to the classical tradition is manifest. In sum, then, *Christus Triumphans* is a fascinating, although admittedly flawed, amalgam of divergent dramatic traditions brought together by Foxe as an experiment in academic comedy. The record of its printings in the sixteenth century and its revival as a school text in the seventeenth century indicate that Foxe's experiment was not altogether unappreciated during the Renaissance.

Foxe as Preacher

Suring his own lifetime, Foxe was much better known as a popular and powerful preacher than as a dramatist. Although he held back from moving into the Anglican establishment and accepting an ecclesiastical appointment which would have entailed regular preaching duties, the record of Foxe's preaching activities is fairly constant, beginning with his residence as a tutor at Reigate in the 1540s and spanning four decades. During his exile, he preached regularly at Frankfort, and after his return he served by invitation as a visiting evangelist in several dioceses, and, again by invitation, he was selected by the bishop of London to preach twice at Paul's Cross, the most important pulpit in England. Of the multitude of sermons Foxe preached during his career, he chose to publish only the two most famous. The first, a Good Friday sermon delivered at Paul's Cross in 1570, was published in two editions the same year as *A Sermon of Christ Crucified* (subsequent editions were called for in 1575, 1577, 1585, and 1609; the English text was so popular that a Latin translation was published in 1571); the second, *A Sermon Preached at the Christening of a Certaine Jew,* appeared in two English and one Latin editions in the year of its delivery, 1578. Both are powerful evangelical sermons marking important and spectacular events of the Elizabethan years.

The Good Friday sermon at St. Paul's would have attracted a large crowd in any year, including the mayor and various civic officials decked out in their robes of office,[10] but in 1570 the St. Paul's sermon took on special importance because of the recent bull of Pope Pius V excommunicating Queen Elizabeth and absolving her Catholic subjects from allegiance to her. A refutation and strong statement of Protestant principles was wanted, and Edmund Grindal, bishop of London, turned to his old friend and fellow exile, the famous martyrologist. This occasion helps to explain the heavy use of antithesis and distinction as rhetorical and logical devices in the sermon; Foxe seeks not only to celebrate the meaning of the Atonement consummated by the crucifixion, but to contrast clearly Catholic and Protestant understanding of the event. Thus, Foxe aims to "awake the hartes" of slothful Christians, in "these drowsie dayes of carnall securitie," even intending "for the Papistes cause to doe them some good."[11] This the preacher will do by illustrating the inadequacy of the Catholic stress only on the *animalis homo,* the physical suffering of Christ which leads to a false veneration of the wood and nails of the cross, showing instead the right way to apprehend Christ crucified, for "it is not sufficient to stay in these outward thynges: we must go further then the sensible man, we must looke inwardly with a spirituall eye into spirituall thinges" (*E,* A4ᵛ).

Foxe's contrasts between Catholic and Anglican responses to Christ's sacrifice are dispersed through an order close to that of the "modern" style of sermon construction in the Renaissance.[12] In this popular Elizabethan mode of sermon organization, the parts of the classical oration are amalgamated with the school rules of Aristotelian logic. Both of Foxe's extant sermons reflect this basic scheme composed of a dedication, stressing the theme, here including an exordium or protheme on the need to know rightly Christ crucified and concluding with a prayer, and the sermon proper divided into two parts. Each part again contains an introduction to the theme, followed by the division, customarily distinguishing the topic into three parts, leading into the discussion and applications of the theme until the final prayer for Christ's church. Stylistically, the sermons also reflect the popular

Protestant bias toward the plain style, although, as in the *Acts and Monuments,* Foxe displays a tendency toward syntactical looseness and, when seeking to move as well as instruct his audience, a florid style aiming at vivid pictorial and sensuous representation. Indeed, because of his subject, the mystery of God's death, he requires extraordinary expression, drawing on the arsenal of rhetoric; Foxe explains: "Now, what thys reconciliation is, and what great thinges come thereof, it followeth likewise to be considered. Which albeit can not so amply be described to you as it is in it selfe, yet by similitudes and examples partly it may be conceaved" (*E,* 28).

Of the various "similitudes and examples" employed in the *Sermon of Christ Crucified,* a particular rhetorical stratagem made Foxe's sermon one of the most famous of its age. Having explained the meaning and the doctrine of the Atonement in Christian theology, Foxe brings on Christ himself to present the message dramatically in an imagined address of Christ from the cross to his vanquished opponents, Sin and Death. The oration, labeled by a marginal note as a *prosopopoia,* is a splendid and arresting stroke; no less interesting are the similarities between this section of Foxe's sermon and the artistic strategies of the *Acts and Monuments.* As Christ speaks of the one greatest enemy he has overcome, Foxe himself enters his discourse to set the stage:

> But before I beginne to speake of this enemy, I will first here play *Ioseph ab Arimathea,* and reverendly take down the body of our Lorde from the Crosse and lay him in his sepulchre, till ye shall heare of hym within these iii. dayes more againe.
>
> And here now having taken down the crucified body of Jesus from the Crosse, to occupy your eyes, and to delite your mindes, I entend, by the grace of Christ crucified, to set up here in Paules Crosse, or rather in Christes Cross, an other Crucifixe, a new Crucifixe, a new Roode unto you, a Crucifix that may do all Christen hartes good to behold. This Crucifixe is he that crucified all mankinde, and hath brought many a man to the gallowes, to the Crosse, to the gibbet, and at last crucified Christ our Savior also. So severe was he, that he spared none; so strong, being armed with Gods justice & judgement, that none could escape him. And now shall ye see him hanged up, and crucified him self: the meryest and most happiest sight, that ever came to man. . . . Ye muse peradventure and marvell what great Crucifixe this should be. . . . (*E,* 113–14)

Here reminiscent of the *Acts and Monuments* are not only the skillful word-painting of this deposition from the cross, but also the fervor signaled by the author's psychological projection into the great drama he describes, the telescoping of time and place, and the deft utilization of suspense, as his audience ponders what greater enemy man might have than Satan. Foxe soon reveals this ultimate enemy to be God's severe law, and, in another vivid metaphor, he transforms the passive figure of Christ hanging upon the cross to a dynamic one of struggle and triumph, dramatically showing the audience the meaning of the Atonement:

And thus have ye upon one Crosse ii Crucifixes, ii most excellent potentates that ever were, the sonne of God, and the law of Godde, wrastling together about mans salvation, both cast down and both slaine upon one Crosse, howbeit not after like sort. First the sonne of God was overthrowen, and tooke the fall, not for any weaknesse in him selfe, but was contented to take the foyle for our victory. By thys fall, the law of God in casting him down, was cast in his owne trippe and forgot him selfe. (*E*, 115)

If eternal victory is assured through Christ's sacrifice, however, temporal triumph is not; thus Foxe concludes the sermon by forsaking eschatology to remind his audience of the immediate perilous situation of God's church on earth:

Onely a litle angle of ye weast partes yet remaineth in some profession of thy name. But here, alacke, commeth an other mischief as great, or greater than the other. For the *Turke* with his sword is not so cruell, but the Byshop of *Rome* on the other side is more fierce and bytter agaynst us, sturrying up hys Byshops to burne us, his confederates to conspire our destructiō, setting kynges agaynst their subiectes, and subiectes disloyally to rebell agaynst their princes, and all for thy name. Such dissension and hostilitie Sathan hath set amongest us, that *Turkes* be not more enemyes to Christians, then Christians to Christiās, Papistes to Protestantes. . . . (*E*, T3^v)

Having instructed and moved his audience to wonder at the miracle of the Atonement and its promise for mankind, Foxe now stirs them to defend their church and state, Fortress Albion, against the circle of enemies who would destroy them. In his concluding prayer for Christ's church once universal but "now driuen into a narrow corner of the world" (*E*, T2^r), Foxe prays for its deliverance from evil and the ultimate conversion of the enemies of the church, including Pope and Turk. Bishop Grindal could not have asked for a more effective and timely performance than Foxe delivered.

A Sermon Preached at the Christening of a Certaine Jew is a literary legacy from one of the spectacular public events of the Elizabethan era, the public conversion and baptism of one Nathanael, a Spanish Jew, in Lombard Street in 1577. A great throng turned out for the event, which featured a speech by Nathanael and a sermon by Foxe. As Foxe had contrasted Protestant doctrine with Catholic in the sermon on *Christ Crucified,* on this occasion he surveyed the grounds of controversy between Christian and Jew, stressing "the principall groundes and foundations of our Christian faith, of the true & syncere church" (*E,* C2ᵛ).¹³ Thus, as in the *Acts and Monuments,* Foxe returns to a survey of the authority and traditions of apostolic Christianity, distinguishing God's true church from its Old Testament forebears and its subsequent modern perversion by Roman Catholics.

The most striking feature of the *Certaine Jew* sermon is its size; in the 1578 English edition, it is 195 pages in length. While the spectacle in Lombard Street might have been an all-day affair, calling for a lengthier sermon than at Paul's Cross where two hours was the accepted maximum, Foxe certainly did not preach all that found its way into print in the sermon. Instead, he expanded on his oral text, adding digressions, amplifying material, and providing supplemental citations and evidence, until he can, with some justice, refer to the work as "this little treatise" (*E,* viiʳ).¹⁴ Yet it retains the marks of oral delivery, and the essential structure, again that of the "modern" sermon form, is clearly discernible beneath the amplifications and additions.

Foxe takes as his text a passage from St. Paul in Romans 11; Foxe explains that "The maner and kinde of his instruction here, wherein hee resembleth the Church of God to an Olive tree, is metaphorical, and propheticall. Which Olive tree consisteth of three partes: Of the roote, of the stocke, and of the branches" (*E,* A5ᵛ⁻ʳ). These correspond, respectively, to Abraham and the Holy Patriarchs of the Old Testament, to the church scattered over the earth, and in the branches sprouting with new life, to the flourishing church of the gentiles in the latter era. As St. Paul had spoken metaphorically, so does Foxe as he offers to combat the Jews with their own weapon, in this case the Old Testament, to prove the justice and truth of Christianity.

It remayneth nowe, that we treate of the promises of the Prophetes,
whereupon you boast so much, and rayse all your building, which only thing
of all others, doeth unioynte and shyuer in pieces all the strong bulwarkes of
your unbeliefe, even to the very bottome of the foundation. And to the ende I
may make this appeare more evidently, I wyll combate a crashe with you in
your owne castle, whereunto I will use none other furniture, but your owne
weapons, I mean the very words and knowen sentences of your owne
prophets. And I wil so deale with you in this cōflict by the ayde and assistance
of God, as not heaping together out of all the Prophets in generall their whole
armorie of proofe that I know, for that were unmeasurable. But I will chuse
rather out of certaine of thē, not a multitude, to surcharge you wᵗ nomber,
but certaine special testimonies, in the which as in choise shot and powder, I
will so batter yᵉ bulwarks of your blūdered unbeliefe, that you shall not be
able by any meanes possible to delude the matter with caffling, nor escape by
denyall, nor with any subtile legerdemayne of litterall exposition, cast a
myste before mine eyes, nor untwyne your selues out of the meashe by any
crooked conveyaunce, as you are wont to do, though ye would neuer so fayne,
but either you shall be pervinced willingly to come to reason, or els against
your willes to be confoūded altogether with the manifest light of the trueth.
(E, E6ʳ–7ᵛ)

To drive home his argument—and the *Certaine Jew* is more polemical
than the *Sermon of Christ Crucified*—Foxe employs typology and
prophecy extensively, as promised in the passage just cited. This
process, coupled with a slackening of the metaphorical intensity of the
sermon or treatise, makes the *Certaine Jew* less attractive to modern
audiences than the earlier sermon. Nevertheless, in both sermons, Foxe
proves himself a skilled and conscientious craftsman setting forth the
fundamental tenets of Protestant Christianity in a form designed to
appeal to and move Englishmen of all stations. They provide convincing evidence of Foxe's popularity as a preacher.

Foxe as Pastor

Along with his preaching, another aspect of Foxe's religious activity
occupied much of his time and energy: his pastoral counseling and
charitable works in the city of London. Simeon Foxe records how his
father's house was jammed with clients, some attracted by his reputation for pious wisdom and godly advice, others by the funds given him

by wealthy friends for disposition to the needy. Indeed, the great outpouring of Londoners of all sorts at Foxe's simple funeral Simeon attributes less to his fame as author of the *Acts and Monuments* than to the affection and appreciation of the city folk for his selfless pastoral concern for them. In the nature of things, this sort of work, important as it was, customarily did not lead to publication, but in at least one instance, a particularly severe visitation of the plague in 1563 when people were forbidden to congregate in any place, Foxe took to print to counsel his fellow Londoners to stand fast in their faith whatever God might send them.

In the summer of 1563, Foxe published a little pamphlet entitled *A Brief Exhortation, fruitfull and meete to be read, in this heauy tyme of Gods visitation in London, to suche as be Sicke, where the Ministers do lacke, or otherwise cannot be present to comfort them.* In it he acknowledges and attempts to assuage the fears of his fellow Londoners, urging them to comfort each other as they can and take assurance from the Scriptures of God's benevolence and divine plan. In particular, men should recall the example of Christ and the martyrs, whose innocent suffering won for them places in heaven and still provide a pattern for all:

And thus being armed with the power and strēgth of Christ, passe thorow this storme, be it neuer so rough and sharpe to the fleshe, hauing before your eyes so many examples of good mē which passed the same way before you as the Prophetes, Apostles, and Marytrs of Christ, who in their extremities passed through greater tormentes, some racked, some torne in pieces, some sawen a sonder, some stoned to death, some hanged by one mēber, some by an other, some broyled upon coales, some burned with flamyng fire; whiche they notwithstādyng abid with pacience. But especially casting up your minde and beholding the death of Christ, learne therby to dye and not to feare death, not to murmure agaynst God. For if he did abyde a smarting passion, and that in his middle and best age: thincke your selfe not better than he.[15]

As this passage suggests, the consolation of *A Brief Exhortation* is decidedly Christocentric; through the sacrifice of the Cross and Christ's promises in the gospels, man is assured of victory over death. The metaphoric texture of Foxe's pamphlet reflects this Christocentric focus. Londoners are to be the good soldiers of "captaine Christ," fighting off fear and despair. Having heard the good news of the gospel, the reader should "now labour to applye the same and to exercise it upon your selfe: wherby lyke a good scholer nowe you may declare by your own doyng, what you haue learned by hearing" (B, 4). The injunction to become Christ's soldier and his scholar is a prelude to Foxe's striking use of biblical paradox and rhetorical inversion. He redefines death for the timorous Londoners, offering, as in the *Acts and Monuments,* a different perspective upon it to minimize the importance of "the bodyly death, seing it is a separation not from the favour of god, but only from the fruition of this present worlde, [therefore] it hath nothing greatly to be feared" (B, 7). He proceeds to elaborate the inversion of man's fear of a death which is actually life and vice versa:

For what is the estate and condition of al men but mere mortalitie; That is to saye, not so soone borne to this worlde as dead to god. And what doth it skill then when a dead man dieth, whiche is dead already before he begynneth to dye: whether to dye sooner or later: as all men be which be borne of Adam. For where Christe sayeth in the gospell, let the dead go burye the dead: what meaneth he, but that we shoulde understande thereby no difference to be betwene them that be dead, and thē that be a liue. . . . (B, 6–7)

The consolation provided by Christ's words and the right perspective upon death which they provide extend even to those most innocent among the victims of the plague: the children. Thus, Foxe concludes by appending "A Prayer to be sayd ouer children, visited by Gods hand with sicknesse, in this sorowful tyme of Gods visitation" asking the intercession of Christ, who summoned the little children to him when he was on earth, and counseling the parents to accept God's will patiently with full faith in Christ the mediator and advocate:

And forsomuche as the paynes of the same poore childe seeme greuous and vehement, we besech thee so mitigate the vehemencie thereof, that by the relieuyng of it, we also may be comforted, dealyng with it according as it shall seeme good to thy divine wisedome, whether by death to call it or by life to restore it, so that whether it goe, or tary, it may be thine, and at last with thine elect be made partaker of that blessed resurrection, whē thou shalt appeare. . . . (B, unpaged)

This little pamphlet is a moving document of pastoral succor. And if, as J. F. Mozley speculates on the basis of a letter from his friend John Parkhurst alluding to Foxe's "visitation at God's hand in this time of mortality," Foxe himself lost one of the young daughters born to him during his German exile in the plague of 1563,[16] the prayer for parents is an especially poignant memorial to the wholeness of Foxe's faith.

Chapter Five

The History of the History: Foxe and the Modern Reader

The Early Printing History of the *Acts and Monuments*

As Simeon Foxe wrote in his memoir, the most distinctive feature of his father's life is Foxe's impressive record of "bearing continually true and solid fruits"[1] from the tracts and translations of the 1540s to the biblical commentary on which he was working at his death. In the four decades of his active publishing career, Foxe turned out a prodigious quantity of material, varying widely in quality and importance from literal translations and assorted service work to original literary productions as diverse as sermons and stage comedies. With only a small handful of notable exceptions, however, few of the miscellaneous fruits of his industry have attracted much modern attention. Instead, Foxe's reputation, like his very name, has been linked inextricably with the one indisputably great work of his lifetime of labor: the *Acts and Monuments*. The critical fortunes of this book from Foxe's day to ours follow an erratic course reflecting the intense emotions stirred by Foxe's record among both his supporters and detractors.

Because Foxe did not intend his great work to speak only to historians, antiquaries, and the intelligensia, he somewhat ruefully relinquished the Latin of the early continental editions to publish the *Acts and Monuments* in English from 1563 on. The book was meant to move the English mind, to prove a case and defeat an opponent in the public arena by marshaling reams of historical data. It is a work, as we have seen, born in controversy, and for the four centuries of its English printing history it has seldom failed to stir the coals of controversy and to provoke strong partisan reaction. Thus the literary history of Foxe's book down through the centuries, the changing times and varied formats of its republication, and the reaction of the English public to the work are of far more interest than the publication record of most great historical works of a more narrow scholarly or noncontroversial nature.

The publication history of Foxe's book is a broad and engrossing topic, encompassing more than a hundred English editions and abridgments. Over a century ago John G. Nichols wrote of being overwhelmed by all the material he was collecting toward a projected work on "The Literary History of the Book of Martyrs," but neither Nichols nor anyone else ever published such a study.[2] Thus, with no pretense at exhaustiveness, I will trace the course of the *Acts and Monuments* as a living text adopted, reshaped, and presented in various literary guises during subsequent centuries under the editorship of professed friends and admirers. These editions usually provoked fusillades of protest and countercharges from Foxe's detractors, ideological and scholarly; indeed, by the dawn of the eighteenth century, in assorted abridged editions the *Acts and Monuments* had taken on a life of its own as a weapon of religious controversy. By the nineteenth century, the *Acts and Monuments* created sufficient controversy to keep several presses, Protestant and Catholic, almost exclusively occupied turning out editions and defenses and attacks upon it. Even a partial survey of this printing history will suggest the important role of the *Acts and Monuments* in English social and popular culture and will help explain why so invaluable a primary record of a crucial period in English history was brought into such low repute and comparative neglect for much of the twentieth century.

Although the power of Foxe's narrative is acknowledged by critics of all persuasions, the *Acts and Monuments* is seldom read primarily for its literary value. Because of its sensational subject matter and frankly propagandistic aims, the *Acts and Monuments* was embraced and speedily elevated to canonical status by English Protestants. They were actively encouraged by the Anglican ecclesiastical establishment, whose response to the partisan message and stirring stories was so strong as to make Foxe's work one of the most influential English books ever written. The importance of Foxe's book was recognized as quickly in Rome as at Canterbury, and a campaign to discredit Foxe's version of ecclesiastical history in general and his account of the recent Marian persecution in particular began shortly after the first English printing of the book. In addition to the sniping of such Catholic controversialists as Thomas Harding in his *Rejoinder to Jewel* (1567), the Roman Catholic counterattack during the Elizabethan era was spearheaded by Nicholas Harpsfield, writing as Alan Cope, in his *Dialogi Sex* (1566) and the Jesuit Robert Parsons whose *A Treatise of Three Conversions of England* (1603) "remains the *locus classicus* of the anti-Foxian case."[3]

Of course, Foxe and his book hardly lacked defenders in Protestant England. Even in the strained religious climate leading up to the civil war, Anglicans minimized their discomfort at the stories of tradesmen following their consciences and Bibles alone even to the stake and Puritans skipped lightly over Foxe's insistence on royal prerogative in religious matters, his steadfast support of the English church as an institution, and the fact that Foxe's chief stories often featured bishops as heroic martyrs. Indeed, both major Protestant religious factions publically proclaimed the virtues of Foxe's book which, as Paul Christianson illustrates from seventeenth-century sources, could be used effectively to support either Protestant position.[4] Precisely because of its effectiveness as propaganda, editors of the seventeenth and eighteenth centuries began offering to the public popular abridgments of the *Acts and Monuments* under various titles, with new prefaces in place of Foxe's to point up the work's agreement with whatever particular stripe of Protestantism the current editor favored.

The original rationale for these abridgments was the expense and bulk of the complete editions, which grew from the two volumes of the late Elizabethan editions to three folio volumes in the 1610 and subsequent seventeenth-century editions. In the first abridgment of Foxe's book, by Dr. Timothy Bright in 1589, the editor justifies his labor "because it is a booke that concerneth so manie, who by reason of the charge of price, and largeness of volume, cannot, either for want or business, enioy the full benefite of the same, I thought good to abridge the historie in such sorte as the benefite and vse thereof might the farther be communicated."[5] As a conscientious editor, Bright protests that he does not seek to supersede "the large Booke: which I doe exhort thee (gentle Reader) the rather for my Abridgements sake, to buy, and vse. For, as the copiousness of that notable worke, hath hid the riche treasures of the same, through charge of price, and mens affaires: so this my labour may geve thee an assay, and appetite, to know further, whereof thou maist here take (as it were) the taste."[6] In fact, Bright's popular edition, shrunk to approximately 800 pages and bound

duodecimo without illustrations, is markedly superior to most subsequent abridgements. Bright eliminates much of the supporting
documentation, hortatory letters to and from martyrs, and other
ancillary material while remaining faithful to the main outlines and
proportions of Foxe's narrative. In addition, Bright's abridgement is
also notable for the excesses it avoids: there are no inflammatory
prefaces or backmatter, no lurid or sensational additions or illustrations, and Foxe's language is reproduced accurately insofar as possible.
Although from Bright's day to ours perhaps a hundred abridgments of
Foxe's book have appeared, it is not until the mid-twentieth century
with George A. Williamson's one-volume edition that another abridgment rises to the level of Bright's.

Along with four complete editions of the *Acts and Monuments,* the
seventeenth century spawned various novelty abridgments, such as
independent publication of individual stories from Foxe with particular
political or moral application to the contemporary scene or such
curiosities as an alphabetical collection of Foxe's martyrs. This latter
publication is particularly interesting for its editor's comments on how
the public read Foxe's history. In his preface, the editor explains the
utility and purpose of his rehandling of Foxe:

And as to the manner of the Epitome, an Alphabetical method, both as to
sufferers and Persecutors, seemed most apt for thy reaping advantage. The
reasons moving the Epitomizing the voluminous works of the author were
these:
   1. Because many who probably would read those greater Volumes, either
cannot acquire them being scarce, or cannot purchase them being dear, or
perhaps have not time to peruse them being great, to occur all which this
abstract may suffice.
   2. The Chief things in these Volumes desired by the Vulgar (whose
instruction is chiefly designed hereby) is the Lives and deaths, the Constancy
and Comforts of the martyrs, which here are briefly contained as to the most
remarkable Martyrs ever since Christ's time; which being portable, may
serve as a Manual to be oft in our hands to be perused, till we get their
experiences on your hearts.
   And although in these *Halcyon* dayes of the Church (which God long
continue) these endeavours may seem to some supervacaneous; yet if we
consider that while we are in the World we must expect troubles, it is no
small prudence to prepare for it.[7]

If the editor's market analysis of his readers' taste is correct, the seventeenth-century reader was not only reading Foxe's work as hagiography rather than history, but the hagiographic appeal was so strong as to obviate the sort of hysterical appeals to the "present danger" provided as rationale for most eighteenth- and nineteenth-century editions.

Thus, Restoration and eighteenth-century editors were interested less in Foxe's work as an ecclesiastical history than as a martyrology, and they cut away historical portions, especially Foxe's material on the Middle Ages, to emphasize the sensational incidents of torture and death. As these editions were abridged on the one hand, so they were expanded on the other by the addition of new, contemporary material such as the Gunpowder Plot of 1604, the Irish massacre of 1641, and so on down to the accounts of the martyrdom of missionaries in the Far East in Victorian editions. At the same time his book was dismembered, Foxe had his language frequently "improved" by editors and the old woodcuts were replaced by new, graphic, and sensational engravings. Thus, by the eighteenth century, Foxe's book has, in effect, passed into the hands of Protestant zealots concerned less with his meticulous tracing of history than with the book's effectiveness as inspired propaganda in kindling anti-Catholic sentiment in England by recalling the events of the Marian era. To this end, publishers sought ways of minimizing the price and popularizing the text so as to bring it within the reach of every Protestant Englishman. For example, one early eighteenth-century publisher thought of selling the work piecemeal in sheaves, as he explains in a preface which emphasizes the nationalistic aspects of the work:

This valuable Book of English Martyrs being grown so very scarce, as to be rarely found but in the Closets of the Learned or Curious, it is hoped that the Method taken to restore it to the Publick, will meet with general Approbation and Encouragement; as it seems to be the most proper Way for promoting the universal Good intended: For the Purchase of so voluminous a Work cannot be reach'd by every one's Purse at once; and therefore this Expedient was resolv'd on, of publishing a certain Number of Sheets weekly, by subscription that the common People might be also enabled, by degrees, to procure it.[8]

In its publication by sheets containing stories of individual martyrs, this eighteenth-century edition anticipates such ventures as the paperbound *Foxe's Book of Martyrs,* twenty-four pages of sensational stories melodramatically illustrated with pictures and photos of martyr memorials, published by the Protestant Truth Society in 1920 to sell for two pence.

At least one enterprising eighteenth-century editor proposed another solution to the challenge of reducing the price of so useful and timely a work to encourage mass readership: a public subsidy to defray printing costs. In a fervent assertion echoed from the eighteenth century to the twentieth by generations of zealous Protestant editors, the Reverend Mr. Madan argues in the preface to an edition of 1776 that Roman Catholicism is no less a danger in later times than in the mid-sixteenth century and Foxe's record of the Marian period is the best educational tool available to alert the English public to Catholic perfidy and iniquity. The Reverend Madan warns his public that "Should any endeavor to persuade thee, Reader, That Popery now is different from what it was in the reign of queen Mary, thou mayst answer, Yes, there is the same difference as between a lion chained up, and a lion let loose. Popery does not burn Protestants to death in Smithfield now, because it hath not power, but it does burn them in Spain and Portugal, because it hath. Be assured that Popery is always the same, and so will continue, until it shall cease out of the earth."[9] Given this proposition, it thus seems self-evident to the Reverend Madan that the publication and dissemination of Foxe's history is of primary importance in stemming Catholicism, even to underwriting publication by the national treasury: "'Twas doubtless with this view that our wise forefathers ordered Mr. Fox's three books to be chained to a desk in some conspicuous part of the parish-churches in this land, that all the parishioners might have recourse to them, and read therein: and I can't help thinking, that it would do honour to those in power, if a law was made to re-publish the whole, at the public expense, and fix them as heretofore for public perusal."[10] There is no record, however, of the Exchequer displaying any interest in the Reverend Madan's public-spirited proposal.

Another eighteenth-century abridgment, misleadingly entitled *Fox's Original and Complete Book of Martyrs,* affords a good example of the additions frequently attached by editors to bring Foxe's account up to date. The title page of this edition promises "A Full Account of The bloody Irish Massacre, The martyrdoms of the missionaries in China, The Barbarities exercised in America, the late Persecutions in France . . . With a great Number of Cruelties exercised against the Glorious Christian Martyrs, not related in any other Work of the Kind whatever."[11] And the editor, identified only as "A Minister of the Gospel," delivers over 100 folio pages of post-sixteenth-century material ranging from the persecution of the Quakers to the great fire of London (a papist plot, naturally), and seventeenth-century persecutions on the Continent down to such current events as the trial and acquittal in 1780 of Lord George Gordon, president of the London Protestant Association, on charges purportedly rigged against him by desperate Catholics. These additions helped the common reader identify himself with the heroic martyrs of Marian England, for as the editors continually remind him, the enemy is the same and unchanging. And the additions preserve and continue the popular journalistic appeal of the original *Acts and Monuments,* which told stories of events fresh in the minds of Englishmen, stories of their relatives, their neighbors, their monarch, and their ministers. Whereas Foxe in his expanded editions had sought to show an unbroken continuity from the sixteenth-century Protestant martyrs back to those of the Roman arena and apostolic days, the editors of the eighteenth- and nineteenth-centuries chopped and compressed the stories of the early martyrs, endeavoring instead to emphasize the nationalistic theme by stressing the continuity of English martyrs and Reformation principles from the days of Henry VIII and his children to the present.

Acts and Monuments in the Nineteenth and Twentieth Centuries

With the advent of the nineteenth century came a new impetus for Catholic emancipation and the liberalization of English law to recognize the rights of English Catholics to full status under the law. Not surprisingly, the conservative Protestant backlash to this movement included a new round of abridged editions of the *Acts and Monuments* featuring prefaces, appendixes, and additions by conservative Protestant ministers which, in their grave premonitory warnings, reflexive anti-Catholicism, and emotional appeals to the English people not to unleash a tide of unscrupulous papists upon the nation, are more rabid than anything Foxe himself actually wrote. For example, an abridged edition of 1803 includes the following perfervid exhortation, which begins by praising Foxe, moves to a harangue against Catholics, and ends in a calculated play upon the deepest fears of the common Englishman:

> The *protestant* cause is under great and lasting obligations to this man. His work exhibits popery in its *own colouring*; and by faithfully shewing what a *popish* government *once* did in this country, proves what a papist government would *again do,* were it set up in these lands; for that vile and wicked system is precisely the same in the nineteenth century it was in the sixteenth; it is still unchanged. In its nature it is still intolerant and cruel—in its operation, tyrannical and oppressive; ruinous to the circumstances, destructive to the lives, and fatal to the souls of all those who are brought under its dominium. Britons! Protestants of all sects and parties! magnify God, who has saved you and your country from this cruel scourge. Join heart and hand in supporting to the uttermost your SACRED CONSTITUTION, one glorious principle of which is, that it is fundamentally *opposed* to popery in all its principles, in all its serpentine windings, and Proteus forms and fashions. Remember with horror and execration that Molochian system that burnt your forefathers, their wives and infants, in the flames, because they would not adore a *wafer god.* . . . Watch, diligently watch against the restoration of this worst of all governments. Were popery to have the upper hand once more in the state, it would deluge the nation with blood: such is its vindictive, unvarying, and invariable nature.[12]

In editions such as this one, Foxe and his ecclesiastical history are little more than a tool to club Catholics, and what is left after Foxe's text is abridged and his language "improved" is chiefly the most gruesome of the sixteenth-century stories of martyrdom. And this cut text is usually hedged about by prefaces, afterwords, appendixes, and the like driving home the nature of the "present danger." The 1803 edition is typical in encircling the text with appendixes on "Errors of the Romish Church" (arranged under such topic headings as "Strange and inhuman Maxims held by the Papists"), "The Danger of Tolerating Popery," and an epilogue entitled "Some Concluding Remarks" which duplicates both the substance and tone of the preface.[13] The appearance throughout the century of Foxe's narrative, or pieces of it, in a context of such Catholic-baiting and religious demagoguery further undermined academic respect for Foxe and his labors. It became easy for scholars to dismiss Foxe's history as being as biased and emotional as its latter-day partisans obviously were, and so Foxe was tarred and feathered by the excessive zeal of his champions. In fact, in these eighteenth- and nineteenth-century editions it is often difficult to tell what is canonical and what the later editor has added. Typically, once a reader negotiates the thicket of prefatory and appended material in an edition of 1803, he finds the editor has further tagged to Foxe's truncated history not only a spate of post-sixteenth-century stories of martyrs at the rear but also a narrative of the pre-Christian martyrs from Abel down through the Old Testament at the front, both additions blending directly into Foxe's text.

Indeed, an editor with a strong sense of the dramatic could himself take credit for having saved England from the bloodbath Catholic enfranchisement would surely bring, as the Reverend J. Milner did in 1807 in an edition reprinted frequently in the nineteenth century. In his preface, Milner observes that "It is now scarcely a year since the imminent danger which threatened the established Church of this happy kingdom, induced the Editor of the present volume to come forward, and exert his humble efforts to counteract it. . . . he felt himself imperiously called upon to come forward . . . and boldly to PROTEST against the emancipation of Catholics."[14] Forewarned of the Catholic push for enfranchisement, Milner reveals "he was resolved to contribute his feeble efforts to effect their overthrow. . . . One opportunity, it occurred to him, he should find by publishing a new Edition of Fox's Martyrs."[15] According to Milner's account, his projected edition stirred so much public interest and enthusiasm that it created a climate in which Catholics, afraid to wait for publication of a book which would rouse the Protestant public against them, moved too early on their scheme to liberalize restrictions on Catholics, as Milner reports with glee:

The alarm was immediately sounded; the Editor was accused of exciting the prejudices of the *ignorant multitude*; for so the abettors of the Catholic claims were pleased to denominate the reflecting Protestant Christians of our realm; and the men who dared to propose to his Majesty, to violate his Constitutional oath, by admitting Catholics into the army and navy, with the same privileges, and upon the same terms as Protestants, BROUGHT THEIR PLAN *prematurely* BEFORE THEIR SOVEREIGN and the public, lest the effects which the Protestants were making, should circumvent the objects that the Catholics had in view. Their failure and overthrow . . . are yet too fresh in the memory of the public to need any comment.[16]

Here Foxe's history has become a mere adjunct to current political in-fighting, reported in breathless tabloid prose.

In the absence of some actual evidence of perfidy on the part of nineteenth-century English Catholics, one would expect the editorial cries of alarm cited as motivating factors in the republication of Foxe's narrative to lose credibility with the reading public. In fact, Victorian editors shift emphasis and strategy while continuing to manipulate fears of the Catholic peril. An abridged edition of 1814, "Revised and improved by the Rev. John Malham," illustrates the change in tactics. The Reverend Malham is almost apologetic in his preface that the Catholics have not committed any recent atrocities or outrages in England, thereby depriving his edition of the timeliness exploited by the Reverend Milner and other earlier editors. Hence, he must resort to warning the public against the future threat and known propensities of Catholics:

Of the great expediency of disseminating, as much as possible, the history of martyrdom, as exercised by papists on protestants of different denominations, in times comparatively modern, we are fully convinced. We may assure ourselves, that the present depressed state of popery in England is no proof that its leading principle has been abandoned, though this assertion has often been sounded in our ears. We cannot possibly doubt of its still lurking on the hearth in obscurity, in readiness to blaze out on stirring up the embers; and that it only wants a fostering-hand to blow up the coals, and to re-kindle the sparks into an over-powering flame. That popery has now become an innocent thing, and perfectly harmless, is a sentiment which, we acknowledge, we cannot persuade ourselves to subscribe to; and when our readers have attentively perused the contents of this volume . . . we shall only desire them to lay their hands on their hearts, and tell us whether, in their conscience, they can really entertain an opinion that the tenets of the latter are so very innocent, as some unthinking politicians would induce them to believe.[17]

The stress here and in subsequent Victorian editions falls on the value of the *Acts and Monuments* as a predictive work, an accurate map of England's future should vigilance ever slip. To enhance the immediacy of this appeal, extra attention is devoted to post-sixteenth-century stories of Protestant suffering at Catholic hands, here gathered in an appendix entitled "A Summary of Persecutions which Protestants have sustained from the Malignity of the Papists in the times generally subsequent to the Narrative of Mr. Fox's History." A key feature of this section of modern martyrdoms is a set of engravings commissioned for the edition. The visual impact of the original woodcuts of Foxe's early editions, ranging from the realistic to the allegorical, was a vital element in the success of the work. In particular, the pictures of Protestant saints confidently standing amid the flames praising God drove home visually Foxe's central message and served a positive devotional purpose. By contrast, the new engravings for the Reverend Malham's edition are frankly sensational, visual catalogs of horror calculated to shock, titillate, and outrage in just about equal proportions.

An example of these inflammatory Victorian engravings is a lurid diptych entitled "Horrid Scenes in the Irish Massacre in the year 1641." The upper engraving is a visual anthology of torture, with a male Protestant in the center being savagely scourged with rods by one torturer while stretched bound over a wheel (probably breaking his back), with another torturer egging on a large wolflike dog to chew the right hand of the victim, thrown out in distraction at his suffering. Above and in the center of the engraving, a Protestant female, probably the wife of the supine victim, is lashed to a post while a Catholic torturer affixes large metal pinchers to her exposed breast, which he is about to remove. She throws back her head, twisting away from her tormentor, staring upward in horror, her mouth open. In the background, from left to right illuminated by firelight, a naked Protestant is dragged to death behind a horse, another, hanged by the neck, dangles from a gibbet over an open fire, while on the right yet another victim is being burned alive at the stake. The accompanying engraving on the lower panel completes the image of Protestants perishing by fire and steel by illustrating a scene of Protestant families, prominently including women, children, and infants, being put to the sword and dropped off a bridge into a river below.

Thus the exploitation of Foxe's book takes a decisive turn toward the sensational in the popular editions from the second decade of the nineteenth century on. The engravings of Malham's edition are copied and imitations appear in a number of Victorian editions, affording the reader the emotional stimulus formerly provided by citations of contemporary Catholic sedition and alarums of imminent peril. Mid-Victorian editors followed this successful format and concentrated upon attractively packaging their abridged editions. In stark contrast, an edition of 1837 is aimed at women and children, its language sanitized to suit Victorian mores.[18] The following year, the Reverend M. Hobart Seymour published a two-volume edition which he proudly proclaimed as a "Family Edition," explaining that "owing to the state of society in the age in which this work was written, there was a coarseness of expression, and an absence of delicacy and propriety, in some of the narrations, which render it unfit for family perusal, in the present state of society, and which have aided much in consigning the work itself into oblivion. All these narrations, and indelicacies, have been most carefully expunged from this edition."[19] Seymour's edition, frequently reprinted as one of the most popular Victorian versions of the *Acts and Monuments,* is notable for the apocalyptic rhetoric with which the editor describes the Catholic menace, held back only by a few great works such as Foxe's and the vigilance of English Protestants:

> This state of things is pregnant with the most disastrous consequences to the Protestantism of England. . . . Shall it be, that the souls of our children, and our children's children, shall become the merchandize of Friars, and their morals become contaminated by the Priests of the Confessional? . . . It were better that the blast of death should sweep through the land, and as of old, leave the first-born dead in every house; and that the wail of the desolate, and the cry of the mourning should be heard on every wind, and echoed from every home, than that a calamity so disastrous as this, should befall our father land. Then, indeed, would the dark spirit of Popery be traced by the fall of our fanes and the ruin of our altars; and she would erect her throne amidst the fallen columns—the crumbling arches, and the mouldering aisles of the Temple of Protestantism.[20]

Here, perhaps, in Seymour's heavily freighted metaphors, is a verbal equivalent of Malham's lurid engravings.

Meanwhile, handy duodecimo abridgments were published steadily throughout the century, usually with some such standard justification as that offered by the editor of an 1839 pocket editon: "Our aim and our motives, in the publication of this imperishable work, in its present cheap and conveniently compressed form—a work whose history and circulation demonstrates its qualifications, for affording efficient and valuable co-operation in the holy duty, and now absolutely necessary work, of resistance to the avowed, uncovered, unconcealed designs and ambition of the popish clergy, and the popish political agitators and leaders of the day—will be inferred, and sanctioned."[21] The year 1855 saw the appearance of another pocket-size condensation, with a preface by the clerical secretary of the Islington Protestant Institute arguing that persecution is both essential and natural to the Catholic church, while the Christian Book Society published an even briefer pocket edition of only 125 pages in 1870. Another of these popular pocket editions contains a preface by the bishop of Carlisle congratulating the publisher for bringing out another edition of so necessary a work: "The 'Book Society' does wisely, when in the days of Victoria, it strives to outvie the Reformers of the sixteenth century. For it would place a copy of the Book of Martyrs, not indeed in every church, but in every house, yea, and in every hand. And is there not a cause? Rome is labouring, with redoubled effort, for the subjugation of Britain. She attacks us openly from without, while there are traitors ready to open our gates from within. And the people have forgotten that she is a siren who enchants but to destroy."[22]

This goal, a copy of Foxe in every hand, is pursued into the twentieth century in editions such as the illustrated paperbound pamphlet *Foxe's Book of Martyrs* published from 1920 to 1954 by the Protestant Truth Society and the pocket edition published by the Book Society in 1931. This latter edition contains a preface by Jesse Sayer which reechoes the familiar Victorian warning: "As this age draws to its close there is no doubt that persecution in a very severe form will take place. Those who side with Christ and refuse to give way to the Spirit of the Anti-Christ will have to suffer."[23] Finally, it is both fitting and significant to conclude this survey of the popular publication history of Foxe's book by observing that the only abridged editions of Foxe's book now in print are popular paperback ones without notes but with pious prefaces, editions in no way different from those of a century ago.[24]

The Historical Case Against Foxe

One of the most interesting features of the early popular tradition of abridgments is that they neither encouraged nor provoked critical historical examination of Foxe's text. Instead, during the seventeenth and eighteenth centuries, Foxe's book was generally praised by Protestants and condemned by Catholics without any serious examination of the controverted matter beyond Foxe's defenses of himself against Harpsfield's charges and Parsons' attack upon the book, both of Elizabethan vintage. As the nineteenth century dawned, however, Catholic apologists and sympathetic historians reviewed the ancient charges against Foxe, checked them against the traditions and evidence of the Counter-Reformation, and launched a new attack upon the *Acts and Monuments* and its most zealous partisans. The success of this assault besmirched Foxe's reputation for almost a century.

One of the first in the field paving the way for an attempt to refute Foxe on historical grounds, using the evidence of selected historical inaccuracies in Foxe's book to argue the invalidity of his entire record, was the Catholic priest and antiquary, John Milner. In 1798, the Reverend Milner published his two-volume *History, Civil and Ecclesiastical, and Survey of Antiquities, of Winchester.* Through a study of the county history of the Winchester district, Milner hoped that by refuting Foxe's account in this one quarter, he could thoroughly discredit the *Acts and Monuments.* At the same time, Milner copied the broadbrush attacks of Harding, Parsons, and the Tudor controversialists, arguing that Foxe's book "which has been the store-house for all succeeding writers on the same subject, has been demonstrated to be one tissue of falsehood, misrepresentation, and absurdity."[25] His defense of Tudor Catholicism and his attack on Foxe's history expands in succeeding years from Winchester in the Marian era to Foxe's entire book and its premises in such subsequent works of Milner's as his *End of Religious Controversy* (1818) and his frequently reprinted *Letters to a Prebendary.* In his letter on "Persecution" in the latter volume, Milner offers a vivid witness of the success of the popular abridged editions of the *Acts and Monuments* which zealous Protestant divines were rushing to the presses:

I have had frequent opportunities of observing, that amongst the many foul caricatures of the religion of our ancestors held up to public view, that which exhibits it as a sanguinary system, supported by swords and muskets, and surrounded with racks, gibbets, and fires, is the one which has been chiefly successful in inflaming the minds of Englishmen with hatred against it and its professors: a hatred which they do not entertain for the unbaptized Quaker, or the antichristian Socinian, and which has sometimes led them into the extremities of cruelty, from the mere hatred of cruelty. Those who feel an interest or a pleasure in exciting this odium, are fully sensible of its fatal efficacy. Hence, they are never weary with ringing the changes on the names of John Huss, and Jerome of Prague, on the massacre of Paris, and especially on the fires of Smithfield. For the same uncharitable purpose, we find the lying *Acts and Monuments* of John Fox, with large wooden prints of men and women, encompassed with fagots and flames in every leaf of them, chained to the desks of many country churches, whilst abridgments of this inflammatory work are annually issued from the London presses, under the title of *The Book of Martyrs.* [26]

Milner's objections to Foxe's book and "its fatal efficacy," even when taken out of the context of county history, expanded, and included in popular polemic form in *Letters to a Prebendary,* were apparently still too erudite or expensive for many working-class Catholic readers. In order to bring these historical doubts about Foxe to the common reader, the Reverend T. Baddeley, a Catholic priest from Manchester, published an inflammatory handbook in dialogue form setting forth conservative Roman Catholic positions and blasting Protestantism in all its forms and doctrines. In *A Sure Way to Find Out the True Religion, in a Conversation between a Father and His Son* (1820), a small paper-bound pamphlet meant to sell for two pence, Baddeley devoted ten of his 95 pages to an assault on Foxe in the following vein:

S. You said that all the saints, who are gone to heaven, lived and died Roman Catholics. Pray does not Fox's Book of Saints and Martyrs show, that there are many Protestant saints as well as Catholic?
F. Fox's Book of Saints and Martyrs is full of lies; for "there is scarcely one whole story in that huge volume, but which is falsified and perverted one way or another." There were found on two leaves of Fox's Book one hundred and twenty lies. . . . [27]

In Baddeley's modern catechism, invective is blended with attempts at factual refutation of Foxe, a pattern which becomes the standard form in Victorian rebuttals to the *Acts and Monuments*. Thus Baddeley lists a number of Foxe's martyrs from the early Tudor period asserting that they were condemned and executed not for religious but for civil crimes. Hence, the wise father trumpets victory over superstition to his son:

> Thus, we have gone through six months of Fox's calendar, and I have not mentioned one quarter of his falsehoods; the other six months are quite as bad. You see then, what a book this is, which Protestants boast so much of. These saints of his were nothing but a bunch of deluded, rebellious, impious, and blasphemous wretches, most of them put to death by the law of the land where they resided for their crimes. Many of them were condemned for their lewd lives, conspiracies, rebellion, and murder; some for witchcraft and conjuring; others for sacrilege and theft, and even for flatly denying Christ himself. In fact, "to call a man one of Fox's saints, is become the same as to call him a great rogue." What a pretty set of saints, then, are those to boast of! Surely every sensible Protestant must be ashamed of such saints as these. So much, then, for this famous, or rather infamous, book of saints and martyrs.[28]

Even as Catholic controversialists published inexpensive pamphlets and tracts seeking to steady their flock and raise doubts among the general public who were snapping up abridged editions of the *Acts and Monuments,* their historical arguments paled beside the immediate visceral impact of the riveting engravings which decorated the editions of Foxe. Inflammatory engravings, such as those of Malham's edition, were a special target of the Reverend George Haydock in *A Key to the Roman Catholic Office; Briefly Shewing the Falsehood of Fox's Martyrology* (1823). Haydock deplored modern Protestant editors of Foxe who

> say, they have "united themselves for the purpose of diffusing among their fellow believers, a knowledge and love of the genuine principles of Christianity; and consequently, a hatred and *abhorrence of the corruptions and crimes of popery and its professors.*" They accompany the work with wood-cuts representing the "cruelties of the inquisition." . . . Persecution was never an article of the Roman Catholic faith. How iniquitous, therefore, must be the project of these *plain christians,* who, though they scruple to our images, or pictures, for the sake of promoting piety, zealously employ them to enkindle HATRED against their Catholic fellow-subjects![29]

Since it was impossible to suppress the inflammatory pictures, however, the next step, as the fiery Catholic printer William Eusebius Andrews realized, was to provide the public with pictures attacking Foxe's reading of ecclesiastical history and supporting the Catholic version. Thus Andrews commissioned and printed a series of engravings to adorn his *A Critical and Historical Review of Fox's Book of Martyrs, Shewing the Inaccuracies, Falsehoods, and Misrepresentations in that Work of Deception* (1824), originally printed and sold in installments at three pence each, then collected into hardback form. The engravings which accompany Andrew's 400-page attempt to refute Foxe range from a print of the devil looking over Foxe's shoulder and encouraging him to write to pictures of Catholics being persecuted by English Protestants both in the sixteenth century and later. Each picture is accompanied by an explanation of the engraving, as Andrews sought to fight fire with fire through sensationally visual as well as verbal appeals to his audience. Meanwhile, his actual historical refutation resembles that of Baddeley in resting heavily upon appeals to Parsons and the anti-Foxe tradition on the one hand and slanted partisan interpretation of previously established facts on the other.

In the late 1830s and through the following decade, S. R. Maitland, the librarian of Lambeth Palace and an archivist with scholarly credentials, began an extensive campaign to discredit the veracity of Foxe and the authority of the *Acts and Monuments* through a scholarly reexamination of surviving documents from the early period. In a host of articles and several books, Maitland drew on sixteenth-century documents to argue that in his account of the Tudor period, Foxe willfully distorted evidence and presented material he knew to be untrue.[30] Indeed, in the 1830s, when Stephen Cattley announced plans to edit a full modern text of the *Acts and Monuments,* Maitland decried and sought to block the project. Failing, he wrote long, hostile reviews of the first volumes of the Cattley text, pointing out errors Foxe had made and Cattley had compounded through clumsy editing. Both Cattley and the Reverend George Townsend, author of the life of Foxe in what is still the most widely available and utilized edition of the *Acts and Monuments* in our time, rather than admitting and restudying the factual problems isolated by Maitland attempted instead a blanket defense of the *Acts and Monuments.* Mozley notes the predictable outcome of this strategy:

"with his two opponents playing into his hands, Maitland gained what appeared to be a crushing victory, and fairly bludgeons them out of the field."[31]

So complete did Maitland's victory seem to be that his researches became immediately the touchstone for devaluing Foxe. Thus, when the Bishop of Carlisle contributed an approving preface to one of the abridged editions of the *Acts and Monuments* in the 1860s, he was immediately taken to task by Father Dominic Trenow, O.P., who censured the bishop for having recommended a work so thoroughly discredited. Concerning Maitland's researches, Trenow argued that "so completely did he succeed in unearthing this Foxe, that though a sedate, studious, and learned scholar and clergyman, he has earned for himself the by no means inappropriate, if not dignified, nickname, of 'Foxhunter.' It may be said with truth, that he ran him to the death, for no one with any literary pretensions has since ventured to quote Foxe as an authority."[32] Thus, on the one hand, Foxe's book was chopped, shaped, and presented to function as a tool of Protestant propaganda whose veracity was automatically assumed among its target audience; and on the other hand, in the academy, the *Acts and Monuments* was often regarded as a work of dubious authority written in the heat of passion by a careless, biased, and intemperate chronicler.

The Present State of Criticism of Foxe's *Acts and Monuments*

The decisive counterblow to the low critical estimate of Foxe the historian was the publication in 1940 of J. F. Mozley's *John Foxe and His Book*. By reexamining contemporary documents and sifting through Foxe's correspondence and records preserved in the British Museum, Mozley was able to devote several chapters to a close study of the charges traditionally brought against Foxe, from Harpsfield to Maitland, including an extensive investigation of key episodes in which Foxe supposedly misrepresented facts. Mozley's book was well received in all quarters and his defense of Foxe and the *Acts and Monuments* widely judged successful. Since Mozley's landmark study, a number of other historians have investigated specific areas of Foxe's record, scrutinizing his historical method and his handling of documents, and while he does not always meet modern standards for historical scholarship, these independent investigations have gone far toward clearing Foxe of the charge of willful misrepresentation of evidence.[33] In sum, since 1940, Foxe's reputation as a careful and accurate, albeit partisan, historian especially of the events of his own day has been cleansed and restored with the result that modern historians no longer feel constrained to apologize automatically for evidence and examples drawn from the *Acts and Monuments*.

With Foxe's reputation in large measure rehabilitated and the seminal importance of the *Acts and Monuments* in the development of the English mind trumpeted by modern studies such as those of William Haller, one might expect a groundswell of scholarly and critical interest in Foxe's great book in our time. However, no such surge of scholarly activity has occurred and therein lies a paradox. Foxe's stature as one of the most influential figures in the English Reformation, the author of one of the greatest English books ever written, is secure; thus, he has a niche of his own in nearly every historical, literary, or ecclesiastical survey of the period. Yet he has attracted far fewer studies than Renaissance authors with far more modest reputations.[34] In particular, there is a curious gap between the enormous impact of Foxe's writings on the English mind, acknowledged even by his detractors, and close studies of the writings themselves. Many modern writers interested in Foxe are doubtless daunted not only by the enormous bulk of the *Acts and Monuments*, which fills eight very substantial volumes in the only complete edition reprinted in the twentieth century, but even more by the lack of adequate and accessible editions; indeed, until proper scholarly editions of Foxe's works appear, the flow of critical commentary is likely to remain slow and tentative.

Additional barriers keep the modern student from an appreciation and critical study of the *Acts and Monuments*. First, there is the matter of Foxe's habits of composition and revision. Because Foxe allowed others to translate from his Latin text major portions of the English editions, the literary critic is often unsure whose actual words he is reading, while the historian is often still uncertain about the reliability of Foxe's facts in any given section of the text as well as bothered by the larger question of the limits of partisan history. In each area, problems seem to conspire to push the potential critic back from the text, with the result that remarkably little criticism of Foxe attempts to come to close quarters with specific episodes in the text. Foxe's various revisions of the *Acts and Monuments* present a problem of equal magnitude. Of the five Elizabethan editions in English, some reflect major revisions, such as the 1570 edition, others only minor ones, as in the 1576 printing, but throughout, Foxe adds, deletes, corrects, and rearranges material while inserting defences of his method into the body of the text and tacking on various prefaces.[35] But none of these editions is today available in print, and as a result, the study of Foxe's textual revisions in the *Acts and Monuments* is an unexplored subject.

Thus unless he is so fortunate as to have access to one of the great library collections which contain a copy of one of the early editions, the modern student has only a 1965 reprint in eight volumes of the second, 1843–49, edition of the widely criticized Cattley edition, the only complete edition of the *Acts and Monuments* published in the twentieth century. This text must be used with caution as it fails to conform to the standards of modern scholarship; rather it adds to and further confuses the problems discussed earlier concerning the texts of the Elizabethan editions.[36] Prompted by Protestant concern at the rising influence and visibility of English Catholics, the Victorian editions prepared by Cattley and, later, by Josiah Pratt of the *Acts and Monuments* aim at readibility; thus the nineteenth-century editions modernize much of Foxe's text, rearrange portions of it, add supplemental and transitional material without regard to the integrity of the text, and select from the various versions of the five Elizabethan editions without attempting either collation or consistency, save for the use of the 1583 edition as the basic copy-text. The resulting text, complete with notes reflecting the editors' strong Protestant bias, is thus a hodge-podge composite unlike *any* of the five complete Elizabethan editions. Thus, the unreliability of the only accessible printed edition of the *Acts and Monuments* is a further deterrent to the study of Foxe. What is needed is a modern scholarly edition of the *Acts and Monuments,* for nothing short of a reliable text of the great work seems likely to stimulate the reevaluation and critical study of Foxe's book for which the studies of Mozley, Haller, White, Olsen, and others have laid the foundation. It is an oddity of modern scholarship that in an age when every minor Jacobean and

Caroline dramatist seems to attract a host of eager editors, John Foxe, for centuries the authoritative interpreter of the English Reformation for Protestants in England and the Commonwealth, can find none. Until this situation is rectified, the lack of reliable and accessible texts will remain the single greatest impediment to the study of Foxe.

Thus the twentieth century has treated Foxe in ambivalent fashion. Sympathetic critics and close scholars have rehabilitated his reputation as an historian and a writer of integrity and force. Also, belatedly, literary critics are beginning to appreciate and explicate the artistry of the *Acts and Monuments*. But on the other hand, Foxe's minor works are largely ignored and unavailable in either modern editions or reprints of old ones. And the great work on which his reputation rests is far more often cited than read by modern critics wary of the only complete text of the *Acts and Monuments* generally available. But the reader who will take the time to follow Foxe through the *Acts and Monuments*, in one of the rare old editions or in the texts of Cattley or Pratt, will rediscover one of the surest guides into the center of the Protestant consciousness in the English Renaissance.

Chapter Six
Conclusion: Old Paths and New Directions

Foxe's immense work, the *Acts and Monuments,* was so successful and important in winning the minds of men that since the sixteenth century not only the great book but its author has been the subject of the most extreme evaluations. To Protestant England he was Father Foxe, if not himself a martyr to the labors of the Reformed religion to which he dedicated his life, then surely a Protestant saint, a beatification well advanced by the time the biography by his son Simeon appeared prefixed to the 1641 edition of the *Acts and Monuments.* To many Catholic readers, however, he was a vile and unscrupulous propagandist, falsifying where he could not slant or warp the record of history. As the preceding chapter illustrates, their denunciations of "Foxe's Golden Legend" containing "more lies than lines" began early, with Nicholas Harpsfield's *Dialogi Sex,* and continued long, down through the work of the Reverend John Gerard in our century. Due to the heated partisan nature of the commentary Foxe's book stimulated, dispassionate critical analysis and evaluation of his work and his achievement is of comparatively recent vintage, almost all of it within the past fifty years.

But as critics discovered Foxe, the public abandoned him. The academy's modern interest in Foxe, the serious scholarly attention so long inhibited by the passions of ideological partisanship, is perhaps a sad certification that his popularity with the English reading public has waned to its lowest point since the original publication of the *Acts and Monuments.* The religious issues that are Foxe's subject matter and that kept his book at the center of controversy a century ago have cooled now in our more secular age. While there is no sign of a large-scale revival of interest in Foxe among scholars, the fine work of Haller, White, and

113

Olsen, to name but three of Foxe's ablest critics, serves to stimulate a small but steady flow of critical commentary. Nevertheless, for most critics, despite his demonstrated achievement and importance, Foxe will likely remain on the fringes of the English literary Renaissance, at least until an accessible and reliable edition of his works is compiled and published.

This study has focused primarily on the *Acts and Monuments,* showing its firm conceptual structure built upon a reordering of historical events to reflect the apocalyptic time scheme Foxe derived from his study of the Bible. For all its great length, it is not a work which ever escapes the controlling intelligence of the author. His management of narrative sequence and his dramatic powers are the equal of his skill in controversy and polemical writing. If stretches of the *Acts and Monuments* seem dull to the modern reader, it is not that Foxe has gotten lost or is belaboring the obvious; rather, he seeks to appeal to an audience that enjoyed controversy, the well-built argument, and the skillful rebuttal. To insure that his central message struck home, Foxe uses repetition as a primary device. The cosmic conflict between Good and Evil and their worldly agents, the struggle between the True and False churches, and the great moral chasm between persecutors and martyrs—these primary themes are the structural underpinning of Foxe's apocalyptic history and he never strays far from them.

If Foxe's management of his enormous prose narrative is impressive, his craftsmanship is no less notable in other features of his great book. Certainly he frequently falls short of his professed stylistic goal of simple and plain speech, but his style in the *Acts and Monuments* is remarkably plastic and adaptable to quick-paced stories told in economical prose, complex twisting sentences to trace subtle doctrinal distinctions, and marvellous dialogue suited to the character and station of the speaker. Indeed, Helen C. White truly observes of Foxe's ear for speech patterns and skill at character delineation that "the pungent dialogue of the Elizabethan dramatists seems less of a miracle after one has read page after page of dialogue and dramatic narrative [in Foxe that is] as brilliant as anything written for the stage."[1] Analysis of other features of Foxe's craftsmanship reveals his biographical strategy in dealing with major and minor figures in the narrative, utilizing repetition and patterning to suggest the symbolic character of his martyrs' actions, while individualizing them through concrete, detailed description. And the survey of the strange publication history of Foxe's book from his own day to ours suggests the answer to the question how such an invaluable primary record of a crucial period of English history fell into such low repute among students and scholars. As chapter 5 illustrates, Foxe's friends almost as much as his enemies must shoulder the blame for the decline in his critical fortunes during the late nineteenth and early twentieth centuries.

There is much more that needs to be done with Foxe; modern critics have taken only the first harvest. There are the minor works; most of them have not been reedited or republished since the sixteenth century. And despite the interest of the last few decades, we have yet to understand the full impact of the *Acts and Monuments*. Good studies of one or another aspect of Foxe's craftsmanship in the book are beginning to appear with more regularity, but comparatively little has been done on the enormous impact of the *Acts and Monuments* on the English mind. Following William Haller's lead, historians such as William M. Lamont and Paul Christianson have traced the most prominent ideas in the book through Renaissance religious and political controversy; but what of the function of Foxe's book in contributing to the emergence of a distinct mode of Protestant apperception, a tendency to see life chiefly in terms of heroes and villains, the elect and the lost, God's people and Satan's? Similarly, Foxe's influence on the art of his age is another broad and fruitful topic for study. Various critics have noted the attraction of the *Acts and Monuments* to dramatists, not only because the work is a storehouse of exciting plots but because Foxe's treatment of his material often highlights its dramatic potentiality. Yet studies of Foxe's impact upon nondramatic authors are rare, despite the popularity and high esteem of his work throughout the period. Foxe's book was known by the young Edmund Spenser, for example, years before he attempted, in verse rather than prose, to undertake a similar task of fitting a sprawling narrative through a Protestant conceptual framework to illustrate Christian morality and celebrate England's destiny. Or, on a broader scale, there is the unexplored territory of Foxe's relationship to the artistic trends of his era, in particular the rise of the baroque style in art and literature. The *Acts and Monuments* parallels continental baroque predilections by focusing on a favorite baroque theme, the moment of death, the intersection of this world and the next, hovering over the examination of intense physical suffering which is also simultaneously the seal and sign of spiritual triumph. Recognition of the *Acts and Monuments* as an indigenous storehouse of themes and techniques customarily associated with the baroque style may better account for the rise of interest in that style by English writers and other artists than theories that posit circuitous routes of Spanish and Italian influence into Protestant England.

In sum, Foxe's claims on the attention of all students of the literature, history, and theology of the English Renaissance are formidable. If he is to us no longer "King Sun," the epithet Thomas Fuller bestowed upon him, dispelling the darkness of ignorance by tracing the bright, true thread of Christ's church through the ages, he is still an author whose great book and other works can illumine for us many of the shadowy aspects of the thought and literature of Renaissance culture.

Appendix

As an illustration of the indeterminate state of Foxe's text in both ancient and modern editions, an episode from the story of George Marsh, martyred at Chester in 1555, may be cited. At the conclusion of Marsh's story, Foxe comments on the fate of his chief persecutor, the bishop of Chester, who died shortly after delivering a sermon attacking Marsh as a great heretic and defending his burning. Below are the accounts of the bishop's death as they appear in the first and last English editions to appear in Foxe's lifetime and the same episode as presented in the revised Cattley text of 1849.

1563 edition

In recompence of this his good and charitable sermon, within short time after, the iuste iudgment of god appeared upon the sayd Byshop: who through his wicked and adulterous behauior, was (most shamefully it is to be spoken) burned with a harlot, and died thereof, as credible report hath been made: for euen they, which did speake best of him in this case, cõfessed that he had a hole or sore, in the secrete and privy partes of his belly. And when som of the Bishops secret friendes (whereof two were Aldermẽ of Chester that had sene the dead body) wer gathered together, and minding to deface or discredite the rumour that then was uppon hym, declared the maner of his disease + woũd: wherat one Brassy being then Coroner (and no heretike by the Romish profession) saide wᵗ an othe, that theẽ surely the Bishop was burnt: for he before that time had taken the viewe of a mariner, which died upon the like disease, in euery case had such euidente sores + tokens as the Byshop had: more particularly mighte be sayde touching the last tragedy of this Byshop, and of his whorehunting; but shamefastnesse calleth backe. (*Acts and Monuments of these latter and perillous dayes* . . . [1563], p. 1122)

1583 edition

In recompence of this his good and charitable Sermon, within short tyme after, the iuste iudgement of GOD appeared upon the sayd Byshop: recompensing him in such wise, that not long after hee turned up his heeles

117

and dyed. Upon what cause his death was gendred, I have not here precisely
to pronounce, because the rumour and voyce of the people is not alwayes to be
followed. Nothwithstandyng such a reporte went in all mens mouthes, that
he was burneth of an harlot. Whereupon whether he dyed or no, I am not
certaine, neither dare leane to much uppon publicke speach. Albeit this is
certaine, that when he was afterward searched being dead, by some of his
secret frendes + certaine Aldermen for stoppyng the rumour of the people,
this maydenly Priest and Byshop was foūd not to be free from certaine
appearaunce, which declared but small virginitie in him, and that the
rumour was not raysed up altogether upō naught, amongest the people. But
of this I will stay, + proceede no farther, not because more cā not be sayd, but
because I will not be so uncharitable in defacyng these men, as they are cruell
in condemnyng Gods seruantes to death. (*Actes and Monuments of matters most
speciall and memorable . . . newly revised.* [1583], 2:1484)

1849 edition

In recompense of this his good and charitable sermon, within short
time after, the just judgment of God appeared upon the said bishop,
recompensing him in such wise, that not long after he turned up his heels
and died. Upon what cause his death was gendered, I have not here precisely
to pronounce, because the rumour and voice of the people is not always to be
followed. Notwithstanding, such a report went in all men's mouths, that he
died of a disgraceful disease. Whereupon, whether he died so or no, I am not
certain, neither dare lean too much upon public speech: albeit this is certain,
that when he was afterward searched, being dead, by some of his secret
friends and certain aldermen for stopping the rumour of the people, this
maidenly priest and bishop was found not to be free from certain appearance
which declared but small virginity in him, and that the rumour was not
raised up altogether upon nought amongst the people. But of this I will stay,
and proceed no further; not because more cannot be said, but because I will
not be so uncharitable in defacing these men, as they are cruel in condemning
God's servants to death. (*The Acts and Monuments of John Foxe . . . revised
edition* [1843–49; reprint ed., 1965], 7:53–54)

The 1563 episode has a sequaciousness and detail lacking in the later
version. The bishop's disease is described in detail and the name and
testimony of the Chester coroner are adduced for support, along with
additional evidence of the grounds of the coroner's knowledge of the

marks of the fatal disease. This latter evidence also serves to heighten the enormity of the bishop's sin by suggesting an unfavorable comparison between his morality and that of common sailors, while the description of the bishop's illicit activity as "whorehunting" seems calculated to provoke an emotional revulsion in the reader. In the 1583 edition, supporting detail is deleted, the rhetoric is muted by the excision of the inflammatory "whorehunting," and various qualifiers are added to the original account. Still, there is no question of the nature of the bishop's sin or cause of death. In the 1849 edition, the Victorian editor follows the 1583 text closely without using any of the material from the earlier version of the story. Instead, the punctuation and spelling of the 1583 version are modernized, grammar improved ("farther" becomes "further"), an occasional word slipped in to smooth the syntax ("whether he died *so* or no"), and, in an apparent bow to standards of Victorian morality, the bishop's fatal malady is metamorphosed from Foxe's vigorous colloquial description, "burneth of a harlot," into the vague euphemism of "a disgraceful disease." Given such a range of variants among the early editions and the "standard" modern edition as this representative selection demonstrates, there is need for extreme care in citing from the *Acts and Monuments.*

Notes and References

Chapter One

1. "The Life of Mr. John Fox," in *Acts and Monuments of Matters Most Special and Memorable, Happening in the Church . . . Now again, as it was Recognized, Perused, and Recommended to the Studious Reader, by the Author, Mr. John Fox.* 9th ed. (London: Company of Stationers, 1684), sig. B5^r. Simeon's memoir, first printed in Latin and English versions at the beginning of volume 2 of the 7th edition, 1632–41, also exists in original holograph manuscript in the British Library (Lansdowne 388). Anthony à Wood in *Athenae Oxonienses* and Thomas Fuller in *The Church History of Britain* add some details in their seventeenth-century sketches of Foxe, but they are not always accurate. Much of Foxe's correspondence, both original and contemporary copies, survives in the Lansdowne and Harley collections in the British Library; some of these letters, both English and Latin, are printed as appendixes to the revised edition of the Cattley-Townsend edition of the *Acts and Monuments* (London, 1843–49). More of these letters, to and from Foxe, are reprinted in the collection edited for the Camden Society by John G. Nichols as *Narratives of the Days of the Reformation* (London, 1859). In response to the attacks of S. R. Maitland on the Reverend George Townsend's biography of Foxe prefixed to the first two editions of the Cattley-Townsend edition of the *Acts and Monuments,* Josiah Pratt edited the biography, adding new material, for his revised edition of the Cattley-Townsend text of 1853–68. In the 1877 reissue of this text, Pratt's biography is replaced by a popular one by the Reverend John Stoughton. The *Dictionary of National Biography* entry for Foxe is by Sidney Lee. J. F. Mozley, working from the Foxe manuscripts in the British Library, satisfactorily authenticates the old memoir as the work of Simeon Foxe and corrects numerous biographical points in his *John Foxe and His Book* (London, 1940), the most satisfactory biographical sketch of Foxe to date. V. Norskov Olsen also adds significantly to our knowledge of Foxe's relationship with his fellow reformers in *John Foxe and the Elizabethan Church* (Berkeley, 1973).

2. Simeon Foxe, sig. B5.

3. Ibid.

4. Ibid., sig. B7^v. J. F. Mozley notes that although the printed text of Simeon's biography reads thirty, in the original Latin manuscript (Lansdowne 388), Simeon crossed out thirty and inserted twenty-five.

5. Ibid.

6. Quoted in Mozley, p. 23.

7. Anthony à Wood, *Athenae Oxonienses,* 3d ed. (1813; reprint ed., New York: Burt Franklin, 1967), 1:530.

8. Simeon Foxe, sig. C1^v.

9. Ibid.

10. Quoted in Mozley, p. 32.

11. Simeon Foxe, sig. C2^v.

12. Ibid.

13. After the title of William Whittingham's tract of 1575, *A Brief Discourse of the Troubles at Frankfort, 1554–1558 A.D.* Foxe's position and the extent of his role in this controversy are considered in W. Stanford Reid, "The Divisions of the Marian Exiles," *Canadian Journal of History* 35 no. 2 (September, 1968):1–26, and Ronald J. VanderMolen, "Anglican Against Puritan: Ideological Origins During the Marian Exile," *Church History* 42 (March, 1973):45–57.

14. Mozley, pp. 43ff.

15. *The Examination of John Philpot* (1556) was the only one of the martyrs' narratives actually published independently at Basel in accord with this scheme.

16. V. Norskov Olsen also suggests that Foxe's conception of his religious vocation was such that he wished to remain free to preach and evangelize without the formal constraints a position in the Anglican church might impose (p. 15).

17. Ibid., p. 16. Most critics, then, consider Foxe an Anglican with definite Puritan sentiments, as in John T. McNeill's description of Foxe's theological position: "Puritan he was in his position on discipline and ceremonial. But with respect to the ministry and the structure of church government he was decidedly an episcopalian, and he thought of himself as an Anglican in good standing" ("John Foxe: Historiographer, Disciplinarian, Tolerationist," *Church History* 43 2 [June, 1974]:220). For dissenting opinions, see Leonard J. Trinterud, who aligns Foxe with the most conservative of the Puritan groups, designating him a member of "the original anti-vestment party" (*Elizabethan Puritanism* [New York: Oxford University Press, 1971], p. 10) and H. C. Porter, who positions Foxe as an "evangelical Puritan," pressing for Puritan reforms within the Anglican church (*Puritanism in Tudor England* [Columbia: University of South Carolina Press, 1971], p. 9).

18. Quoted in Olsen, p. 8.

19. Simeon Foxe, sig. C3^r.

20. Mozley, p. 141.

21. Leslie M. Oliver dispels the common misconception that the *Acts and Monuments* was required in *all* Elizabethan churches, examining the Canon law and the size of the press runs of the sixteenth-century English editions in "The Seventh Edition of John Foxe's *Acts and Monuments*," *Papers of the Bibliographical Society of America* 37 (1943):243–60.

22. Simeon Foxe, sig. C4^v.

23. Ibid., sig. C4^r.

24. Many critics also follow Mozley in surmising that the unnamed citizen who pleads with John Rogers in 1550 to intercede on behalf of the Nun of Kent sentenced to burn for heresy in the *Acts and Monuments* account is in fact Foxe himself. W. K. Jordan's very brief notice of these instances in *The Development of Religious Toleration in England from the Beginning of the English Reformation to the Death of Queen Elizabeth* (Cambridge: Harvard University Press, 1932) scarcely does justice to the strength or significance of Foxe's opposition.

25. Simeon Foxe, sig. C7^v.

26. Ibid.

Chapter Two

1. See Leslie P. Fairfield, "John Bale and protestant hagiography in England," *Journal of Ecclesiastical History* 24, no. 2 (April, 1973):145–60.

2. *The Acts and Monuments of John Foxe,* ed. S. R. Cattley and George Townsend, rev. ed. (1843–49; reprint ed., New York: AMS Press, 1965), 1:xxv; hereafter cited in the text.

3. *Actes and Monuments of these latter and perillous dayes, touching matters of the Church* . . . (London: John Day, 1563), p. 2.

4. Ibid.

5. Ibid., pp. 8, 11.

6. See Frances Yates, *Astraea: The Imperial Theme in the Sixteenth Century* (London, 1975).

7. Lamont, *Godly Rule: Politics and Religion, 1603–1660* (London, 1969), p. 23.

8. See Hughes's chapter, "The Fate of Heretics," in *The Reformation in England* (New York: Macmillan, 1954), 2:254–304.

9. Frances Yates is a notable exception to this reevaluation of Foxe the historian. By her reckoning, "He is quite untouched by the new critical schools of historical writing . . . he is an old-fashioned chronicler. Though he heaps together great masses of documents, these are not critically investi-

gated but drawn into the great stream of Papacy and Empire patterns in their Protestant and English interpretation. His history of the kings of England is in the straight-forward chronicle tradition . . ." ("Foxe as Propagandist," *Encounter* 27, no. 4 [October, 1966]:80).

10. Levy, *Tudor Historical Thought* (San Marino, Calif., 1967), pp. 102–3.

11. For example, even in the first English edition of 1563, Foxe writes that "we will now proceed (God willing) to the flourishing reign of king Edward, his son, next after him succeeding, requesting by the way and desiring thee, gentle reader, that if anything besides that which is or hath been by us collected hitherto, do come to thy hands, knowledge, or memory, that thou wilt gently impart the same unto us, whereby it may be published hereafter to further profit of many" (5:696).

12. Christianson, *Reformers and Babylon: English Apocalyptic Visions from the Reformation to the Eve of the Civil War* (Toronto, 1978), p. 37. See also F. Smith Fussner's agreement on the same point: "Foxe printed many original sources in his work, and by so doing he made a distinct contribution to historiography. The emphasis on evidence, whether from ancient or modern history, or from printed or unprinted sources, was not news to the humanists and other intellectuals, but Foxe made a point of printing this evidence in the vernacular for the benefit of the common reader" (*Tudor History and the Historians* [New York, 1970], p. 270).

13. Christianson, p. 37.

14. Tucker Brooke and Matthias A. Shaaber, *The Renaissance (1500–1600)* (New York: Appleton-Century-Crofts, 1967), p. 374.

15. For example, J. A. F. Thompson checks Foxe's account of the Lollards against surviving documentary evidence and concludes that "on the whole he emerges with reasonable credit from the investigation, particularly as a preserver of documentary material which is no longer extant" ("John Foxe and Some Sources for Lollard History: Notes for a Critical Appraisal," *Studies in Church History*, ed. G. J. Cuming [London: Thomas Nelson and Sons, 1965], 2:257). "If we must reproach him, it must be not with exaggeration but with incompleteness," A. G. Dickens concurs ("Heresy and the Origins of English Protestantism," in *Britain and the Netherlands,* ed. John S. Bromley and Ernest H. Kossman [Groningen: J. B. Wolters, 1964], 2:53), and in "A Note on the Reliability of Foxe"—an appendix to "Heresy Trials in the Diocese of Coventry and Lichfield, 1511–12" (*Journal of Ecclesiastical History* 14, no. 2 [October, 1963]:173–74)—John Fines defends Foxe's accuracy. Charles C. Butterworth rechecks and confirms the accuracy of Foxe's account of the conversion of Thomas Bilney in "Erasmus and Bilney and Foxe," *Bulletin of the New York Public Library* 57 (1953):575–79.

16. Rupp, *Six Makers of English Religion, 1500–1700* (London: Hodder and Staughton, 1957), p. 54.

17. McNeill, "John Foxe: Historiographer, Disciplinarian, Tolerationist," *Church History* 43 (1974):227.

18. Olsen, p. 19.

19. Foxe relates the story of this dramatic discovery in *Acts and Monuments,* 1:290–91.

20. *An Harborowe for faithfull and true subjectes,* quoted in William Haller, *The Elect Nation: The Meaning and Relevance of Foxe's Book of Martyrs* (New York, 1963), p. 88.

21. See Haller, *The Elect Nation.*

22. Loades, *The Oxford Martyrs* (London: Batsford, 1970), p. 21.

23. Olsen, p. 39.

24. Christianson, p. 9.

25. Lamont, p. 5.

26. Haller, "The Tragedy of God's Englishman," in *Reason and the Imagination: Studies in the History of Ideas, 1600–1800,* ed. J. A. Mazzeo (New York, 1962), p. 27.

27. Helen C. White, *Tudor Books of Saints and Martyrs* (Madison, 1967), p. 2.

28. See, for example, *Acts and Monuments,* 8:657.

29. Haller, "John Foxe and the Puritan Revolution," in *The Seventeenth Century: Studies in the History of English Thought and Literature from Bacon to Pope,* ed. Richard F. Jones (Stanford, Calif., 1951), pp. 209–24 and, in greater detail, in *The Elect Nation.*

30. Parker, *English Reformers,* Library of Christian Classics, vol. 26 (Philadelphia: Westminster Press, 1966), p. 68.

31. Massingham, "John Foxe," in *The Great Tudors,* ed. Katherine Garvin (London, 1935), p. 379.

32. Geraldine V. Thompson, "Foxe's 'Book of Martyrs': A Literary Study" (Ph.D. diss., University of Oregon, 1974), p. 207.

33. After describing the condemnation of two fifteenth-century martyrs by the bishop of Chichester over the question of the exact nature of the bread and wine, Foxe laments that "the knot of amity and concord which was ordained by Christ, to the great comfort of the church (I know not by what means,) through the envy of Satan, is turned into a matter of most grievous discord and dissension among Christians. Insomuch that there hath in a manner no matter continued so many years more pernicious or hurtful unto men's salvation, than that from whence the chief seed or offspring of mortal consolation and comfort of men's life might to be taken and sought for" (3:724).

34. White, p. 179.

35. Yates, "Foxe as Propagandist," p. 82.

36. Loades, p. 8.

Chapter Three

1. See especially Helen C. White's study of the *Acts and Monuments* and the Catholic tradition.

2. Charles Whibley, "Chroniclers and Antiquaries," in *Cambridge History of English Literature,* ed. A. W. Ward and A. R. Waller, (Cambridge: At the University Press, 1967), 3:332.

3. White, p. 159.

4. On the *ars moriendi* tradition, see Mary Catharine O'Connor, *The Art of Dying Well: The Development of the Ars Moriendi* (New York: Catholic University Press, 1942), Nancy Lee Beaty, *The Craft of Dying: A Study of the Literary Tradition of the Ars Moriendi in England* (New Haven: Yale University Press, 1970), and Beach Langston, "Essex and the Art of Dying," *Huntington Library Quarterly* 13 (1950):109–29.

5. See especially the studies of Seymour Byman, "Ritualistic Acts and Compulsive Behavior: The Pattern of Tudor Martyrdom," *American Historical Review* 83 (June, 1978):625–43 and "Suicide and Alienation: Martyrdom in Tudor England," *Psychoanalytical Review* 61, no. 3 (1974):355–73.

6. For example, Foxe describes the terrible martyrdom of John Lambert, adding that the martyr died "after the manner and form that is described in the picture adjoined" (5:236).

7. *Book of Martyrs,* ed. Williamson (Boston, 1966), p. xx.

8. There is an interesting discussion of the iconographical significance of this particular engraving in Elizabeth H. Hageman, "John Foxe's Henry VIII as Justitia," *Sixteenth Century Journal* 10, no. 1 (Spring, 1979):35–44.

9. Mozley, p. 119.

10. According to a story related in Sir John Harington, *A Brief View of the State of the Church of England,* someone thinking to irritate Bonner showed him the engraving of his scourging of a martyr in his garden. Bonner is supposed to have replied with a laugh: "A vengeance on the fool! How could he get my picture drawn so right?" (quoted in Mozley, p. 131).

11. Yates, *Astraea,* p. 44.

12. For example: "As the Lord, of his goodness, had raised up Thomas Cromwell to be a friend and patron to the gospel, so, on the contrary side, Satan (who is adversary and enemy to all good things) had his organ also, which was Stephen Gardiner, by all wiles and subtle means to impeach and put back the same" (5:258).

13. Fr. Philip Hughes's observation on the mindset of the Tudor martyrs is apposite here: "through their habitual frequenting of the Bible, these people have, for themselves, become transformed into Scriptural figures, and all the drama of their lives has itself become, in a way, a Scriptural event, itself a part of, and a continuation of, the sacred story" (2:275).

14. Typical of these references is the following: "Thus, having discoursed things done and past under the reign of king Edward, such as seemed not unfruitful to be known, we will now draw to the end and death of this blessed king, our young Josias" (6:350).

15. *The Ecclesiastical History. Contaynyng the Actes and Monumentes of Thynges passed . . . till the reigne of K. Henry VIII* (London: John Daye, 1570), 1:D$_i$.

16. This representative encomium is from Christianson.

17. For example: "the tragical story and life of Dr. Ridley, I thought good to commend to chronicle, and leave to perpetual memory; beseeching thee (gentle reader) with care and study well to peruse, diligently to consider, and deeply to print the same in thy breast, seeing him to be a man beautified with such excellent qualities, so ghostly inspired and godly learned, and now doubtless written in the book of life, with the blessed saints of the Almighty, crowned and throned amongst the glorious company of martyrs" (7:407).

18. *Actes and Monuments of these latter and perilous dayes, touching matters of the church . . . unto the tyme now present* (London: John Daye, 1576), 1:190.

19. For example, Gina Alexander, "Bonner and the Marian Persecution," *History* 60 (1975):374–91.

20. *Book of Martyrs,* ed. Williamson, p. xxix.

21. White, p. 146.

22. Yates, *Astraea,* pp. 42–50.

23. White, p. 156.

24. Craig, *The Literature of the English Renaissance 1485–1600* (New York: Collier Books, 1967), p. 36.

25. Lewis, *English Literature in the Sixteenth Century Excluding Drama* (New York: Oxford University Press, 1954), p. 300.

26. *Book of Martyrs,* ed. Williamson, p. xiv.

27. One difficulty attendant upon discussion of Foxe's English prose style is the origin of the 1563 text, which encompasses the earlier *Commentarii* translated by others under Foxe's supervision along with much new material added by Foxe himself. Since Foxe reviewed, revised, and took responsibility for both content and style of the English editions, as in his retort to Nicholas Harpsfield writing as Alan Cope, the distinction between the English prose Foxe wrote and the translation he supervised from his Latin may fairly be minimized.

28. *Actes and Monuments of these latter and perilous dayes* . . . (1576), 1:294.

29. Review of *The Elect Nation,* by William Haller, *English Language Notes* 2 (1965):223–24.

30. See Mozley's chapter sifting the charges pro and con concerning Foxe's veracity in the account of the Guernsey martyrs (pp. 223–35). He finds that all available independent evidence supports Foxe's account.

31. White, p. 161.

32. Other examples of this authorial projection include Foxe's account of the disputations involving Latimer and Ridley at Oxford in 1554. Here Foxe becomes so caught up in the struggle between the forces of light and darkness that he distills the charges against the Protestant divines and himself offers a point by point refutation of them, thus psychologically placing himself almost as a participant in the affair, standing shoulder to shoulder with Latimer and Ridley defending God's truth (see 6:520ff.).

Chapter Four

1. Simeon Foxe, sig. B5ʳ.

2. J. H. Smith prints the relevant portions of Foxe's presentation letters along with much other useful background information on the plays in his edition *Two Latin Comedies by John Foxe the Martyrologist* (Ithaca, N.Y., 1973); hereafter cited in the text as *L.*

3. Baldwin, *Shakspere's Five-Act Structure* (Urbana: University of Illinois Press, 1963), pp. 353–56.

4. Mozley, p. 53.

5. Marvin T. Herrick, among others, is skeptical of Foxe's claims of originality: "It is hard to believe that Foxe, for all his assertions of independence, was not influenced by Kirchmeyer's *Pammachius*" (*Tragicomedy: Its Origin and Development in Italy, France, and England* [Urbana: University of Illinois Press, 1962], p. 60n.).

6. In his prologue, Foxe somewhat disingenuously asserts: "It was enough for me, following only the Apocalyptic history, to transfer as far as possible from the sacred writings into the theater those things which pertain primarily to ecclesiastical affairs" (*Two Latin Comedies,* p. 209).

7. See Herrick's chapter "Contributions of the Christian Terence to Tragicomedy" in *Tragicomedy,* pp. 16–62.

8. Blackburn, *Biblical Drama Under the Tudors* (The Hague: Mouton, 1971), pp. 106–17.

9. "In a way, his play is a morality on a grand scale in which cosmic Virtues and cosmic Vices struggle for the soul and body (Psyche and Soma) of man and for 1500 years struggled for the soul of Ecclesia, a tearful, passive, and apparently helpless protagonist" (ibid., p. 109).

10. John Stow has a vivid account of a typical Paul's Cross Good Friday sermon and its audience in his *The Survey of London* (London: Everyman's Library, 1970), p. 151. Millar Maclure says that on special occasions the audience for a sermon at Paul's Cross could run into the thousands in *The Paul's Cross Sermons 1534–1642* (Toronto: University of Toronto Press, 1958), p. 7.

11. *The English Sermons of John Foxe* (Delmar, N.Y., 1978), sig. A4ʳ; hereafter cited in the text as *E*.

12. The term is used by J. W. Blench, who discusses characteristics of this type of sermon construction in his *Preaching in England in the Late Fifteenth and Sixteenth Centuries* (New York: Barnes and Noble, 1964), pp. 71–112.

13. According to the title page, the 1578 English version of the sermon was "Translated out of Latine into English by James Bell." Presumably, Foxe delivered the original sermon in Lombard Street in English also.

14. Foxe had already reworked the sermon once, for delivery to Sir Francis Walsingham, who due to illness was unable to attend the original delivery. Foxe reconstructed it from his notes and delivered it to Walsingham at his home; subsequently, at his encouragement, Foxe printed the sermon with a dedication to Walsingham.

15. *A Brief Exhortation . . .* (London: John Day, n.d.), pp. 4–5; hereafter cited in the text as *B*.

16. Mozley, p. 72.

Chapter Five

1. Simeon Foxe, sig. C3ʳ.

2. *Narratives of Days of the Reformation,* ed. Nichols, pp. xxvii–xxviii.

3. Mozley, p. 227. See also his chapter "Foxe's Book: His Assailants," pp. 175–203.

4. Christianson, pp. 44–45; see also Lamont, p. 35.

5. *An Abridgement of the Booke of Acts and Monvmentes of the Chvrch: Written by that Reuerend Father, Maister Iohn Fox: and now abridged by Timothe Bright, Doctor of Phisicke, for such as either thorough want of leysure, or abilitie, haue not the vse of so necessary an history* (London: I. Windet, 1589), sig. 4²ᵛ⁻ʳ.

6. Ibid., sig. 4³ʳ-4⁴ᵛ.

7. Μαρτυρολογια ἀλφαβετικη, *or An Alphabetical Martyrology . . . Extracted out of Foxe's Acts and Monuments of the Church* (London: R. Butler, 1677), sig. A4-B1ᵛ.

8. *The Book of Martyrs: Containing an Account of the Sufferings and Death of the Protestants In the Reign of Queen Mary the First, Originally written by Mr. John*

130   JOHN FOXE

Fox: And now Revised and Corrected by an Impartial Hand (London: John Hart
and John Lewis, 1732), unpaged [preface].

9. John Fox, *The Book of Martyrs: Containing an Account of the Sufferings &
Death of the Protestants in the Reign of Queen Mary the First. Now carefully revis'd
& Corrected . . . by the Rev. Mr. Madan* (London: H. Trapp, 1776), 1:A1.

10. Ibid.

11. *Fox's Original and Complete Book of Martyrs; Or, an Universal History of
Martyrdom* . . . A New Edition, Now Carefully Revised, Corrected, and
Improved, By a Minister of the Gospel (London: Alexander Hagy, [1782]),
title page.

12. *The Book of Martyrs, or Christian Martyrology: Containing An Authentic
and Historical Relation of Many Dreadful Persecutions against The Church of Jesus
Christ, From the Death of Abel to the beginning of the Nineteenth Century*
(Liverpool: J. Nuttall, 1803), 1:viii.

13. See, for example, the account of the London riots of 1780 when a
Catholic relief bill was before Parliament and the essays "A Refutation of the
Doctrines of the Church of Rome," and "An Essay on Toleration," arguing,
of course, against it, appended to Henry Moore's *The History of the Persecutions
of the Church of Rome: and Complete Protestant Martyrology . . . Including the
Substance of Fox's Book of Martyrs* (London: Brinner and Co., [1810]).

14. J. Milner, *An Universal History of Christian Martyrdom . . . Originally
Compiled by The Rev. John Fox, M.A. And now entirely re-written and corrected,
with many important Additions, and copious historical Notes, Commentaries, and
Illustrations* (London: B. Crosby and Co., 1807), p. v.

15. Ibid., p. vii.

16. Ibid.

17. John Malham, *The Book of Martyrs or the Acts and Monuments of the
Christian Church . . . by John Fox, Revised and improved* (London: Thomas
Kelly, 1814), p. A. Such dire but relatively unfocused warnings may be
paralleled in any of the popular abridgments of the century. See, for example,
an edition of 1850 where even the retreat of Catholicism is presented as
ominous. Here Catholicism, personified as "the man of sin," is described as
"losing much of his power in lands which he has hitherto ruled with a rod of
iron, but he is aiming to redeem his losses in distant regions of the globe, and
is obtaining subtle entrance into the British Isles. Under the cloak of
Jesuitism and the mask of Puseyism, the inveterate foe of God and man is
diligently at work, and may at length boldly show his face even in high
places. The increased circulation of such a work as this may greatly assist in
defeating his plans, and in throwing a fence around our common Protestant
faith" (Ingram Cobbin, *Foxe's Book of Martyrs . . . with Notes, Commentary,*

and Illustrations, by Rev. J. Milner, M.A., A New and Corrected Edition, With an Essay on Popery, and Additions to the Present Time, [London: Partridge and Oakey, 1850], p. iv).

18. According to the editor, one Charlotte Elizabeth, her edition even boasts royal encouragement: "But the voluminous work of Foxe being scarcely suited to very general reading, it was deemed right to furnish the female and the youthful portion of our people with an abstract of what it especially concerns us, as a Protestant church, universally to know. Your Majesty, treading in the steps of your revered royal consort, has been pleased to sanction this attempt likewise . . ." (Charlotte Elizabeth, *The English Martyrology, Abridged from Foxe* [London: R. B. Seeley and W. Burnside, 1837], p. vii).

19. M. Hobart Seymour, *The Acts and Monuments of The Church . . . By John Foxe, A New Edition, with Five Appendices . . . The Whole Carefully Revised, Corrected, and Condensed* (London: Scott, Webster, and Geary, 1838), 1:ix.

20. Ibid., p. vii.

21. *The Beacon: A History of Protestant Martyrdom . . . Originally Composed Under The Title "The Acts and Monuments of the Christian Martyrs" by the Rev. John Fox, M.A. A New Edition, Greatly Improved and Corrected* (London: T. Allman, 1839), p. viii.

22. *Foxe's Book of Martyrs.* Preface by the Hon. and Right Rev. Samuel Waldegrave, D. D., Lord Bishop of Carlisle (London: Book Society, [1880]), p. viii.

23. John Foxe. *The Book of the Martyrs* (London: Book Society, [1931]), p. viii.

24. The only recent edition now in print is *Foxe's Book of Martyrs,* ed. Marie Gentert King (Old Tappan, N.J.: Fleming H. Revell Co., 1968). Two older abridgments are still in print: W. Grinston Berry's *Foxe's Book of Martyrs* originally published by the Religious Tract Society in 1926 and *Foxe's Christian Martyrs of the World* from the Moody Press.

25. John Milner, *The History, Civil and Ecclesiastical, and Survey of Antiquities, of Winchester* (Winchester: James Robbins, [1798]), 1:357.

26. John Milner, *Letters to a Prebendary . . .,* 8th ed. (London: William Eusebius Andrews, [1833]), p. 44.

27. Baddeley, *A Sure Way to Find Out the True Religion . . .* (Derby: Richardson and Son, for the Catholic Book Society, [1820]), p. 43.

28. Ibid., p. 52. Baddeley's attack went through at least nine editions between 1820 and 1884. Its popularity with the reading public called forth several rebuttals defending Foxe and challenging Baddeley's interpretation of

these narratives of martyrs. They include such full-blown efforts as *Popery Unmasked: Being a Full Answer to the Rev. T. Baddeley's Sure Way to Find Out The True Religion: In Which Our Martyrologist, John Fox, Is Defended Against the Author's Misrepresentations; The Errors of Rome Are Detected and Exposed; And the Unaltered Hostility of Popery to Protestantism Is Clearly Evinced* (London: Baldwin, Cradock, and Joy, 1825). The author, the Reverend James Richardson, offers a 470-page counterblast to Baddeley's little book. He challenges Baddeley's interpretation of the facts and accuses him of wilfully misreading Foxe's statements. Predictably, he concludes that "While the candour and honesty of Fox will be admired, and the verity of his narrative confirmed, in the estimation of every one who reads, without prejudice . . . the duplicity and dishonesty of Mr. Baddeley must be despised, and his whole performance loaded with the merited execration of a slanderous libel" (p. 93). A more modest refutation, entitled *A Brief Reply to "A Sure Way to Find Out the True Religion . . .," by A Member of the Reformed Catholic Church,* was published in tract form at a price of four pence in 1841 by the British Society for Promoting the Religious Principles of the Reformation. The author, in replying to the seventh edition of Baddeley's work, is both more concise and more moderate than Richardson; he allows that Foxe "was honest, but he was not infallible." Thus some factual errors are acknowledged to be in the *Acts and Monuments,* although these are affirmed to be minor inaccuracies which do not touch upon the larger credit of the work.

29. *A Key to the Roman Catholic Office . . .* (Whitby: R. Kirby, 1823), p. iv.

30. Much of Maitland's attack on Foxe first appeared as articles in the *British Magazine* during the decade from 1837 to 1847. *Six Letters on Foxe's Acts and Monuments* (1837), *Notes on the Contributions of the Rev. George Townsend* (1841–42), *Remarks on the Rev. S. R. Cattley's 'Defence'* (1842), and *Essays on . . . the Reformation in England* (1849) all first appeared as articles in the magazine and were reprinted separately. Maitland also published *A Review of Foxe the Martyrologist's History of the Waldenses* (1837) and six more *Letters on Foxe's Acts and Monuments* (1837–38) and two essays on "The Personal History of John Foxe" (1843) in the *British Magazine* which he did not republish separately.

31. Mozley, p. 181.

32. Trenow, *The Credibility of John Foxe, the "Martyrologist"* (London: Thomas Richardson and Son, 1868), p. 12.

33. See especially the studies by J. A. F. Thompson, A. G. Dickens, and John Fines cited above in chapter 2.

34. See my survey of modern studies of Foxe, "Recent Studies in Foxe," *ELR* 11, no. 2 (Spring, 1981):224–32.

35. The posthumous 1596 edition, the fifth, contains new material, chiefly from the Tower records, which may have been collected and prepared by Foxe himself between the fourth edition of 1583 and his death in 1587 or which may represent the first of many uncanonical additions to the book by later editors.

36. See the appendix for a concrete illustration of the problems confronting the modern reader who seeks to ascertain and recover what Foxe actually wrote.

Chapter Six

1. White, p. 194.

Selected Bibliography

BIBLIOGRAPHIES

There is no adequate bibliography of Foxe. Over a century ago in *Narratives of Days of the Reformation* John G. Nichols observed that the task of compiling a primary bibliography of Foxe was as formidable as it was a necessary undertaking; unfortunately, however, it is a need which has not been met by modern scholars. To consider only Foxe's most famous book, the two Latin and five sixteenth-century English editions of the work which became the *Acts and Monuments* suggest the dimensions of the problem. Foxe so added, deleted, and rearranged material in each of these editions that a line-by-line analysis and comparison of each would be required for accurate bibliographic description. Then the editions and abridgments of the *Acts and Monuments* from the sixteenth to the twentieth centuries run into the hundreds in England, America, and the Commonwealth. As for secondary literature, the bibliographical essay on Foxe in the "Recent Studies" series of *English Literary Renaissance* (11 [1981]:224–32) by Warren W. Wooden surveys modern critical studies of Foxe. Much briefer bibliographical treatments of primary and secondary Foxe materials may be found in John L. Lievsay, *The Sixteenth Century: Skelton through Hooker* (New York: Appleton-Century-Crofts, 1968) and *The New CBEL* (Cambridge: At the University Press, 1974).

PRIMARY SOURCES

1. Editions of Foxe's Writings
Actes and Monuments of these latter and perillous dayes . . . London, 1563. The
first English edition of Foxe's masterpiece, translating and incorporating most of the Latin forerunners Foxe published on the Continent
during his exile, the *Commentarii rerum* (1554) and the *Ecclesia gestarum*
(1559), with the addition of so much new Marian material that the
folio, at 1,800 pages, is three times the size of *Ecclesia gestarum*.

The Ecclesiastical History, Contaynyng the Actes and Monuments. . . . 2 vols. London, 1570. This edition completes Foxe's plan for the work, extending his historical survey back to the time of Christ. Much new information on the Tudor period is also added along with many new woodcuts.

Actes and Monuments of matters most speciall and memorable, happening in the Church, with an universall Historie of the same. . . . Rev. ed. 2 vols. London, 1583. The last edition revised by Foxe.

The Acts and Monuments of John Foxe. Edited by Stephen R. Cattley. 8 vols. London, 1837–41. Cattley based his text on the 1583 edition of the *Acts and Monuments,* with various additions from earlier editions and modernized, corrected, and rearranged portions of the text. This is the last complete edition of the work; following the attacks by S. R. Maitland, it was revised and reissued in 1843–49. Reprinted in 1965, this is the text found in most libraries. Josiah Pratt revised the Cattley text and the biography of Foxe in volume 1 for republication in two late nineteenth-century printings.

The Book of Martyrs. Edited by George A. Williamson. Boston: Little, Brown, 1966. With a critical introduction, notes, and a glossary, this is the best modern abridgment.

Two Latin Comedies by John Foxe the Martyrologist: Titus Et Gesippus and Christus Triumphans. Edited by John Hazel Smith. Ithaca, N.Y.: Cornell University Press, 1973. The only modern scholarly edition of any of Foxe's works.

The English Sermons of John Foxe. New York: Scholars' Facsimiles & Reprints, 1978. A facsimile edition with an introduction by Warren W. Wooden surveying Foxe's preaching activities and assessing his surviving sermons.

Smith, John Hazel. "John Foxe on Astrology." *English Literary Renaissance* 1 (1971):210–25. An edition of a manuscript tract by Foxe attacking astrology.

2. Letters

Narratives of Days of the Reformation. Edited by John Gough Nichols. London: Camden Society, 1859. Contains correspondence to Foxe concerning the *Acts and Monuments,* the letters transcribed from originals in the British Library and connected by a narrative commentary and notes.

The Remains of Edmund Grindal, D. D., successively Bishop of London, and Archbishop of York and Canterbury. Edited by William Nicholson. Cambridge: Parker Society, 1843. Grindal's correspondence with Foxe during and after their exile is of primary biographical importance.

SECONDARY SOURCES

1. Biographies

[Foxe, Simeon]. "The Life of Mr. John Fox." In *Acts and Monuments of matters most speciall and memorable, happening in the church, with an universall historie of the same; wherein is set forth at large the whole race and course of the church, from the primitive age to these later times of ours, with the bloody times, horrible troubles, and great persecutions against the true martyrs of Christ* . . . 7th ed. 3 vols. London: Islip, Kingston and Young, 1632–41. The only early biographical sketch of Foxe, shown by J. F. Mozley to have been written by his youngest son, Simeon.

Mozley, J. F. *John Foxe and His Book.* London: Society for Promoting Christian Knowledge, 1940. Although not a full-scale biography of Foxe, the biographical sketch contained in this book is the most comprehensive to date, correcting factual errors in both the biographies included in the Victorian editions of the *Acts and Monuments* and the *Dictionary of National Biography.* Mozley's study also includes a description and brief evaluation of each of Foxe's works.

2. General Studies—Books and Parts of Books

Bainton, Roland H. "John Foxe and the Women Martyrs." In *Women of the Reformation in France and England.* Minneapolis: Augsburg Publishing House, 1973, 2:211–30. Surveys the attitude and significance of Foxe's treatment of female martyrs.

Christianson, Paul. *Reformers and Babylon: English Apocalyptic Visions from the Reformation to the Eve of the Civil War.* Toronto: University of Toronto Press, 1978. Traces the impact of the *Acts and Monuments* on both Anglicans and Puritans through early seventeenth-century religious thought and controversy.

Clebsch, William A. "The Elizabethans on Luther." In *Interpretations of Luther,* edited by J. Pelikan. Philadelphia: Fortress Press, 1968. Concentrates on the image of Luther in the *Acts and Monuments* and Foxe's interpretation of Luther's thought so as to make it palatable to English readers.

Dickens, A. G. "Heresy and the Origins of English Protestantism." In *Britain and the Netherlands,* edited by John S. Bromley and Ernest H. Kossman. Groningen: J. B. Wolters, 1964, 2:47–66. Strong defense of Foxe's accuracy in his treatment of the records of Lollard martyrs.

Fussner, F. Smith. *Tudor History and the Historians.* New York: Basic Books, 1970. Good discussion of the dual commitment of Foxe's historical method.

Haller, William. "John Foxe and the Puritan Revolution." In *The Seventeenth Century: Studies in the History of English Thought and Literature from Bacon to Pope,* edited by Richard F. Jones. Stanford: Stanford University Press, 1951, pp. 209–24. Seminal essay demonstrates how Puritan leaders utilized the ideas in the *Acts and Monuments* to combat Archbishop Laud and the royalists.

————. "The Tragedy of God's Englishman." In *Reason and the Imagination: Studies in the History of Ideas, 1600–1800,* edited by J. A. Mazzeo. New York: Columbia University Press, 1962, pp. 201–11. Good discussion of Foxe's influence on John Milton.

————. *The Elect Nation: The Meaning and Revelance of Foxe's "Book of Martyrs".* New York: Harper and Row, 1963. Stimulating and controversial book which argues that the *Acts and Monuments* is a religio-nationalistic polemic designed to win the fervent support of the English for the Crown and the Anglican church.

Hughes, Philip. "The Fate of Heretics." In *The Reformation in England.* New York: Macmillan, 1954, 2:254–304. The most comprehensive modern attack on Foxe as an historian and the reliability of the *Acts and Monuments.*

Lamont, William M. *Godly Rule: Politics and Religion, 1603–60.* London: Macmillan, 1969. Considers the role of the *Acts and Monuments* in seventeenth-century controversy.

Levy, F. J. *Tudor Historical Thought.* San Marino, Calif.: Huntington Library, 1967. Contains a good consideration of Foxe's contribution to Renaissance historiography.

Massingham, Hugh. "John Foxe." In *The Great Tudors,* edited by Katherine Garvin. London: Ivor Nicholson and Watson, 1935. A general appreciation which is strongest on the grounds of Foxe's popularity in the sixteenth century.

Olsen, V. Norskov. *John Foxe and the Elizabethan Church.* Berkeley: University of California Press, 1973. The most thorough study of Foxe's theology and ecclesiology.

Rupp, Gordon. "John Foxe and His 'Book of Martyrs.'" In *Six Makers of English Religion.* London: Hodder and Staughton, 1957. Good, lively general survey.

Thomson, J. A. F. "John Foxe and some Sources for Lollard History: Notes for a Critical Appraisal." In *Studies in Church History,* edited by G. J. Cuming. London: Thomas Nelson and Sons, 1965, 2:251–57. Examination of Lollard documents which confirms the accuracy of Foxe's account in the *Acts and Monuments.*

White, Helen C. *Tudor Books of Saints and Martyrs.* Madison: University of Wisconsin Press, 1967. Extensive consideration of the tradition and literary artistry of the *Acts and Monuments*; an essential study.

Williams, Neville. *John Foxe the Martyrologist: His Life and Times.* London: Dr. Williams's Trust, 1975. Printed lecture that is a good biocritical appreciation of Foxe and his work.

3. General Studies—Periodicals

Battenhouse, Roy W. "Protestant Apologetics and the Subplot of *2 Tamburlaine.*" *English Literary Renaissance* 3 (1973):30–43. Studies Marlowe's indebtedness to the *Acts and Monuments* for both plot and theme in the subplot of *Tamburlaine.*

Brown, William J. "Marlowe's Debasement of Bajazet: Foxe's *Acts and Monuments* and *Tamburlaine,* Part I." *Renaissance Quarterly* 24 (1971):38–48. Studies the method of Marlowe's dramatic reworking of material from the *Acts and Monuments.*

Byman, Seymour. "Ritualistic Acts and Compulsive Behavior: The Pattern of Tudor Martyrdom." *American Historical Review* 83 (1978):625–43. Suggests behavior patterns of Foxe's Tudor martyrs consciously echo those of pre-Nicean martyrs.

————. "Suicide and Alienation: Martyrdom in Tudor England." *Psychoanalytic Review* 61 (1974):355–73. Examines three of Foxe's martyrs for evidence of nonreligious motives for martyrdom.

Dunkin, Paul S. "Foxe's *Acts and Monuments,* 1570, and Single-Page Imposition." *Library,* 5th ser. 2 (1947):159–70. Studies John Daye's method of printing the second edition of the *Acts and Monuments.*

Fox, Alistair. "John Foxe's *Actes and Monuments* as Polemical History." *Parergon* 14 (1976):43–51. Argues for influence of Tyndale on Foxe's idea of history.

Hageman, Elizabeth H. "John Foxe's Henry VIII as *Justitia.*" *Sixteenth Century Journal* 10 (1979):35–43. Examines history and iconography of one of the engravings in the *Acts and Monuments.*

McNeill, John T. "John Foxe: Historiographer, Disciplinarian, Tolerationist." *Church History* 43 (1974):216–29. Studies Foxe's life and writings for evidence on his stand on three major Renaissance issues.

Murphy, Michael. "John Foxe, Martyrologist and 'Editor' of Old English." *English Studies* 49 (1968):516–23. Argues Foxe did not prepare edition of Anglo-Saxon Gospels published under his name in 1571. This essay has important implications for other late works printed as Foxe's.

Nelson, Byron. "The Relationship of Cotton Mather's *Magnalia Christi Americani* and Foxe's *Book of Martyrs* Within the Puritan Epic Tradition." *Bulletin of the West Virginia Association of College English Teachers,* n.s. 3, no. 1 (Spring, 1976):9–20.

Oliver, Leslie M. "John Foxe and the *Conflict of Conscience,*" *Review of English Studies* 25 (1949):1–9. Illustrates how scenes of trial and examination in *Acts and Monuments* influenced a late morality play.

————. "The Seventh Edition of John Foxe's *Acts and Monuments.*" *Papers of the Bibliographical Society of America* 37 (1943):243–60. While focusing on the first three-volume edition, this essay contains a valuable discussion of the printing history of all the early editions of the *Acts and Monuments.*

————. "Single-Page Imposition in Foxe's *Acts and Monuments,* 1570." *Library,* 5th ser. 1 (1946):49–56. Studies John Daye's method of lay-out and printing of the first two-volume edition of the *Acts and Monuments.*

Rechtien, John G. "John Foxe's *Comprehensive Collection of Commonplaces:* A Renaissance Memory System for Students and Theologians." *Sixteenth Century Journal* 9 (1978):83–89. Study of commonplace book published by Foxe, considering its Renaissance context and tradition.

Smith, John H. "Sempronia, John Lyly, and John Foxe's Comedy of *Titus and Gesippus.*" *Philological Quarterly* 48 (1969):554–61. Compares use of a single Boccaccian story by Foxe and Lyly, examining dramatic adaptations and speculating on affinity of two English treatments.

Yates, Frances A. "Foxe as Propagandist." *Encounter* 27 (1966):78–86. Provocative essay argues Foxe is not an innovative historian but "an old-fashioned chronicler" in the *Acts and Monuments.*

————. "Queen Elizabeth as Astraea." *Journal of the Warburg and Courtauld Institutes* 10 (1947):27–82. Reprinted in *Astraea: The Imperial Theme in the Sixteenth Century* (London: Routledge and Kegan Paul, 1975). Discusses importance of conflict between Christian emperors and the papacy as a primary organizational principle in the *Acts and Monuments.*

4. Dissertations

Oliver, Leslie Mahin. "The *Acts and Monuments* of John Foxe: A Study of the Growth and Influence of a Book." Ph.D. dissertation, Harvard University, 1945. The best discussion of the composition and printing history of the *Acts and Monuments* in the Renaissance.

Thompson, Geraldine Vina. "Foxe's 'Book of Martyrs': A Literary Study." Ph.D. dissertation, University of Oregon, 1974. Argues a great debate over the Eucharist is the principal unifying pattern in the *Acts and Monuments.*

Index

272.6
F 795

115470